Is

AEGEAN COAST • CENTRAL ANATOLIA

Jack Altman

JPMGUIDES

Contents

This Way Istanbul   **3**

Flashback   **7**

On the Scene   **17**

    Istanbul   **17**

    Excursions   **32**

    West Coast   **35**

    Central Anatolia   **44**

Cultural Notes   **58**

Shopping   **60**

Sports   **63**

Dining Out   **65**

The Hard Facts   **67**

Index   **72**

Map

Ephesus   40

Fold-out map

West and Central Turkey

Ankara

Istanbul

Old Istanbul

Modern Istanbul

This Way Istanbul

A Foot in Both Worlds

There's nothing simple about Turkey. Asian? Yes and no. European? No and yes. That's the excitement of the place—nothing can be taken for granted. Look at a map of the world and you see a broad expanse of land running along the southern shore of the Black Sea. This is what geographers call Asia Minor and what, since ancient times, has been known as Anatolia ("the land where the sun rises"). At the western end is the narrow strait of the Bosphorus. Cross it and you're in Europe, the continent's southeastern tip.

But you're still in Turkey and this is Istanbul, one of the greatest cities in the world. Eastern or western world? The answer has to be—both. The modern city is the sum of its historical layers, each with a different name—Byzantium for the ancient Greeks and Romans, Constantinople for the Orthodox Greeks and Istanbul for the Turks. Since 1923, when it relinquished its status as political capital to the inland city of Ankara, Istanbul has remained the undisputed cultural and business centre of the country.

Istanbul and its European hinterland represent only 3% of the total land surface. Turkey is roughly the size of all France and Britain together, covering an area of 780,574 sq km (301,380 sq miles). To understand the diversity of Turkey's European and Asian cultural influences, just consider its bordering states: Greece and Bulgaria to the west, Syria and Iraq to the south, Iran, Armenia and Georgia to the east. And north across the Black Sea, Romania, Ukraine and Russia.

All around are the seas. The waters of the Black Sea flow through the Bosphorus and into the Sea of Marmara south of Istanbul, then pass through the strait of the Dardanelles into the Aegean Sea on the country's west coast. Finally they mingle with those of the Mediterranean proper, which bathes the southern coastline.

Fiercely patriotic, the people are also remarkably self-assured, conscious of their long, rich history. This makes them warm and hospitable hosts, in the bazaar, café or restaurant, and especially

P. 1: Ahmet III's dining room, Top-kapı; p. 2 sacred bull of Teshub, the Hittite weather god, Museum of Anatolian Civilisations, Ankara.

3

in their homes. They pride themselves on their Osmanli—Ottoman—origins in Mongolia, but in fact they are now a complex mixture of peoples that have flowed into the country over the centuries from the far-flung territories of the empire in Asia and Mediterranean Europe. Today, about 80% of the population (totalling almost 69 million) are Turks, 20% Kurds. Fully 99% are Muslim, the rest a sprinkling of Greek Orthodox and Armenian Christians, "Latin" Catholics and Jews of Sephardic (Spanish) origin.

Istanbul and the Bosphorus

Physically, Istanbul reflects the multiple currents of its succeeding civilizations. In the historical core, on the European side of the Bosphorus, Corinthian columns and red-brick aqueduct arches evoke its Roman beginnings. Byzantine ramparts, the great St Sophia and other Greek Orthodox churches recall the 11 centuries of Christian rule. The Ottoman Empire is ever present in the Sultans' grand palaces and mosques, some of them rebuilt from churches, and in the Great Bazaar and Turkish baths. In the dilapidated houses along the crowded narrow lanes and alleys of the Golden Horn district northwest of the Old City, Anatolian peasants have replaced the old Jewish and Greek communities.

Beyoğlu, the modern district across the Golden Horn, is distinguished by the elegant neoclassical façades of the Europeans' 19th-century consulates and banks and the functional steel-and-glass architecture of the 20th century. At first glance, the boutiques, art galleries and cafés here could be situated in any modern European city.

Over on the Asian shore, the sprawling suburbs of Üsküdar and Kadıköy offer a fascinating combination of old working-class neighbourhoods rehabilitated by bohemian artists and quiet pockets of Islamic fundamentalists, with new mosques seeming to mushroom on every other street.

Along the Bosphorus waterfront, quiet little fishing villages alternate with grand old 18th-century wooden summer mansions called *yalı* and neo-baroque palaces—now consulates or luxury hotels. On the Princes' Islands in the Sea of Marmara, resorts for the Istanbul bourgeoisie, other handsome summer residences can be seen in peaceful streets delightfully free of motor traffic. In lively contrast, just inland from the Marmara's south coast, is Bursa, the Ottomans' first capital prior to the conquest of Constantinople.

West Coast

Viewed as a broad peninsula, the western region of Turkey is a series of parallel river valleys—the Menderes, Gediz and Bakir—spilling into the Aegean in creeks and coves. The valleys are divided by mountain chains that plunge in steep promontories at the coast and pop up again in the sea as islands. Among them are the near-lying Greek islands of Limnos, Lesbos, Chios, Samos and Kos.

From Istanbul, access to the Aegean Sea is through the long strait of the Dardanelles (Çanakkale Boğazı), focus of fierce fighting in World War I. On the channel's north shore, the fateful coastal battlefield of Gallipoli (Gelibolu) is marked by commemorative monuments and cemeteries of British, Australian and New Zealand soldiers. In ancient times, the strait was protected on its southern shore by the kingdom of Troy (Truva), focus of the Greeks' legendary heroism and treachery. In the on-going excavations, historians and dreamers alike can propose their pet theories.

The scene of the Trojan Wars makes a fitting start to an exploration of the coast that figured so importantly in ancient Greek history. Small fishing ports like Assos and Ayvalık or major beach resorts such as Kuşadası, Bodrum and Marmaris make perfect bases for visiting the archaeological sites and, equally important, just lazing around and enjoying the leisure facilities. Assos (Behramkale) itself still has remains of its ancient city settled by the Greeks in the 8th century BC. Near Ayvalık, Pergamum (Bergama) has a magnificent acropolis.

Just east of the enormously popular resort of Kuşadası is the superb site of Ephesus. This is undoubtedly one of the Mediterranean's best-preserved cities of classical antiquity. On the road south to Bodrum lies another trio of ancient sites—the lovely sanctuary of Priene, the impressive Greco-Roman colony of Miletus and the massive temple of Didy-

1

THE BEST BAZAAR For many a traveller, **Istanbul's Grand Bazaar** (Kapalı Çarşi), the greatest market in Turkey, has no match anywhere else in the world. This vast treasure-trove at the heart of the Old City is a place of adventure that people love to explore many times over.

ma. Bodrum itself is a handsome, dazzling white seaside resort. Originally known as Halicarnassus, it was the home of the great Greek historian Herodotus. Marmaris is another haven for the sun-sand-and-sea set.

From the Aegean coast, you can make an excursion to one of Turkey's most famous sights—the spectacular natural white travertine terraces formed by the mineral pools of Pamukkale. Besides the possibility of a side-trip to the ancient site of Aphrodisias, the journey gives you a feel for the mountainous topography of Turkey's western region.

Ankara and Central Anatolia

The centre of the Anatolian peninsula holds the answers to Turkey's national identity. Over vast expanses of rolling grassland more hospitable to sheep than to man, ancient archaeological sites bear witness to the indigenous Hatti farmers, their nomadic Hittite conquerors, Assyrian traders, Phrygians and Romans. In the towns are the fine mosques of the Selçuk Turks and handsome houses of the Ottoman Empire. It was at the heart of this country that Atatürk, father of the Turkish republic, chose to create its new capital, Ankara. It is a largely modern city, made more lively by its thousands of university students than by its politicians and diplomats. It has some good restaurants, bars and cafés, but above all, one of the country's finest archaeological museums with a rich collection devoted to the Hittites.

The not-so-glittering Golden Horn separates Old Istanbul from the modern city.

Flashback

Stones, Bones and Pictures

The country's history, or rather its prehistory, began with the remains of a giant barbecue left in upland caves north of Antalya around 8000 BC: a few charred fragments of animal skeletons, stone weapons used to hunt the wild beasts, flint blades to skin them and cut them up—plus engravings of their images on the cave walls.

By 6500 BC, the hunters and gatherers of fruit and nuts had been replaced by farming communities scattered across the Anatolian plateau. The people lived in tight clusters of mud-brick houses on stone foundations, such as the village of Çatalhüyük excavated southeast of present-day Konya. They produced wall-paintings with the bull's head emblem, brightly polished pottery, and terracotta fertility goddesses, broad-hipped and big-bosomed.

Merchants from Mesopotamia and Assyria led their caravans across Anatolia to the Bosphorus, trading their textiles and tin for Cappadocian copper. They appreciated, too, the local Hatti people's decorative pottery. More valuable than the exchange of goods was the commerce in knowledge. Foreign techniques in irrigation were traded for Anatolian know-how in metallurgy.

Trojans and Hittites

Along the Aegean coast, trade and piracy increased links with the western world, with one community in particular attracting the attention of the Greeks and subsequently capturing the imagination of the world: the kingdom of Troy. Strategically positioned at the entrance to the Hellespont (Dardanelles) and so commanding access to Black Sea trade via the Sea of Marmara, Troy began its rise to wealth and fame with a first settlement in the 3rd millennium BC. Archaeologists have traced nine separate layers of city development before it sank into oblivion at the end of the Roman Empire around AD 400.

The Trojan War waged by the Greek adventurers of Homer's *Iliad* (Troy also bears the Greek name Ilion) most probably occurred around 1260 BC. But the famous hoard of jewellery, gold and silver plate identified by the 19th-century German amateur archaeologist Heinrich Schliemann as the "treasure of King Priam" in fact dates from a much earlier period, around 2500 BC, clearly a heyday in Trojan prosperity. Writing—the Sumerians' cuneiform (wedge-shaped) script —was introduced by Assyrian merchants from the Mesopotamian region between the Tigris and Euphrates rivers. (The two great waterways have their sources in the mountains of eastern Anatolia.)

Meanwhile, the Anatolian heartland to the east had come under the control of the Hittites invading from the north, most likely from across the Caucasus mountains. After conquering the Hatti, they ruled a powerful empire that lasted from 2000 to 1200 BC, but did not impinge on the trading centres of the Aegean coast and European Thrace. They established their capital at Hattuşaş (modern Boğazkale) north of Cappadocia. The Hittites were lenient and open-minded for their time, notably egalitarian in rights of men and women. A king and queen shared the throne, while slaves were allowed to marry and maintain private property.

Greeks and Persians

The Trojan conflict was only one episode in a long period of wars and catastrophes, encouraging Greek communities to colonize the coasts of Asia Minor around 1000 BC. The region north of Smyrna (Izmir), gradually embracing Troy and Pergamum, was settled by Aeolians from the Greek mainland. The central region from Smyrna to the Meander river (modern Menderes), including Ephesus and Miletus, was colonized by Ionians from the Athenian hinterland of Attica and the Cycladic Islands. The southern coast encompassing Halicarnassus (modern Bodrum) was settled by the Dorians, Greece's tough conquerors from the Balkans.

At the tail end of this colonization, in the 7th century BC, traders from Megara on the Corinthian isthmus laid the first stones of modern Istanbul—beginning with Chalcedon (now suburban Kadıköy) on the Asian shore of the Bosphorus. According to ancient legend, it was known as the "city of the blind" because its inhabitants had not seen the more advantageous site on the European shore—which would be founded soon afterwards, in 660 BC, as Byzantium by a Greek named Byzas. The settlements remained a quiet backwater for the next thousand years.

Smyrna, too, remained little more than a village until Roman times, but other Aegean cities achieved considerable fame.

Miletus was a formidable sea power, establishing colonies on the Black Sea and spearheading Greek settlement in Egypt. Traders peddled its highly esteemed woollen goods and furniture throughout Europe and western Asia. The great scholars of Miletus included Thales (636–546 BC), the first known Western philosopher, pioneer in geometry and accurate predictor of eclipses; Anaximander (611–547 BC), who originated cosmic ideas of the infinite and eternal and anticipated evolution theories in seeing man's origin in the fish; and geographer-traveller Hecataeus (540–480 BC), whose map-making covered eastern Europe, Asia and Africa.

Ephesus rivalled Miletus in commercial energy, swelling its coffers with lucrative tourist trade from pilgrims visiting the great temple of birth-goddess Artemis. It, too, had its renowned philosopher, Heraclitus (535–476 BC), who inspired modern existentialists with his statement: "You cannot step twice into the same river, for fresh waters are ever flowing in upon you."

This wisdom came too late for the fabulously wealthy but over-ambitious Croesus. Having annexed much of the Aegean coast to his inland kingdom of Lydia, he tried to expand eastwards, too, but the Persians were more than he could handle. In 546 BC, they devastated his grand capital of Sardis and made satrapies of the Aegean ports and Byzantium. An Ionian revolt led by Miletus was crushed, and the coastal towns served as launching pads for the all-out Persian attack on Greece. Typically, Halicarnassus, birthplace of Greek historian Herodotus, had to participate in King Xerxes' invasion fleet in 480.

For nearly two centuries, the Aegean cities were pawns in the Athenians' struggles with the Persians and then the Spartans. Each warring party in turn extracted heavy contributions to its treasury in exchange for "protection" against the enemy of the moment.

Alexander Passes Through

In 334 BC, when the Persian Empire was once more in control of the eastern Aegean, Alexander the Great, king of Macedonia, crossed the Dardanelles onto the shores of Anatolia. With a well-thumbed copy of Homer's *Iliad* in his pocket, the 21-year-old soldier made first for Troy to pay homage to his heroes Achilles and Ajax, whom he considered his Greek predecessors in the conquest of Asia. In rapid succession, he took the Persian dependencies of Sardis, Ephesus, Miletus and Halicarnassus, giving each of them governments of Greek democracy. The expedition continued eastwards and inland before Alexander scored a vital victory over King Darius III at Issus on the road to Syria. To commemorate this battle, he

9

founded a city—known later as Alexandretta (Iskenderun).

After his death in 323 BC, Alexander's successors carved up the conquered lands. Most of Anatolia was absorbed into the larger Babylonian empire of Seleucus. Its western rim on the Aegean coast was dominated by the resplendent kingdom of Pergamum, which prospered from silver mines, textiles, rich agriculture and cattle breeding. Under the Attalids, a dynasty of philosopher kings who were also brilliant patrons of the arts, Pergamum became dazzlingly beautiful, famous for its school of sculpture and a monumental library second only to that of Alexandria.

In response to the jealous Egyptian capital's export-ban on papyrus, Pergamum's books used a material that derives its modern name from the town's name: parchment.

Enter the Romans

In 133 BC, probably to prevent an unruly populace taking it away from his family, Attalus III bequeathed Pergamum to the Romans, the new strongmen in the eastern Mediterranean. As a first foothold in what they called *Provincia Asia*, wealthy Pergamum proved a lucrative windfall to local governors. But neighbouring rulers were less accommodating. King Mithradates VI of Pontus (on the south coast of the Black Sea) rose against this imperialist exploitation and in 88 BC reputedly massacred 80,000 Roman men, women and children.

Enter St Paul

From AD 40 to 56, another Anatolian troublemaker, the apostle Paul, made his way through the country preaching the Christian message of Jesus, first to fellow Jews and then more successfully to the Gentiles. From his home town of Tarsus near the Syrian border, he carried his mission not only to neighbouring Mediterranean ports at Perge, Antalya and Myra, but also up the Aegean to Miletus, Ephesus, Smyrna, Sardis, Pergamum and Troy. Helped by the Roman network of paved roads, Paul also travelled inland to Hierapolis (Pamukkale) and Antioch.

Rise of Constantinople

Throughout classical antiquity, Byzantium shared with the Aegean ports the ever-changing fortunes of war among the rival powers of Greece, Persia and Rome. After a short-lived attempt to break away from Rome, Emperor Septimius Severus destroyed the town in AD 196 and rebuilt it with the Hippodrome at the centre.

Elegant gateway at the top of the Street of the Curetes in Ephesus, the best-preserved of Turkey's ancient cities.

The city's strategic position on the Bosphorus, commanding access to the Black Sea, became a key factor in the 4th-century struggles to control the eastern half of the Roman Empire. Constantine defeated his rival Licinius at Chrysopolis (present-day Üsküdar) on the Asian shore of the Bosphorus and made Byzantium his capital. It was inaugurated under the name Nova Roma in 330, but everyone preferred to call it Constantinople.

Together with new city walls to enclose seven hills in an analogy with Rome, Constantine gave the city a superb palace, imperial baths, a forum and several churches to underline his support for the Christian religion. Although Constantine considered Christianity to be a moral force superior to Rome's pagan cults, he saw in it chiefly a useful expedient to impose unity on his empire; he was baptised only on his deathbed in 337. When Rome finally fell in 476, Constantinople remained capital of the Eastern, henceforth Byzantine, Empire.

Over the next five centuries, peace was never prolonged. The city was subject to constant barbarian invasion, fire and plunder. During these formative years of Christianity, theological dispute gave rise to bloody civil wars. In 11

532, after full-scale revolt ended with the massacre of 30,000 rebels in the Hippodrome, Justinian instituted sweeping legal reforms and rebuilt the city, in particular a new and more splendid St Sophia (the first was inaugurated in 360 under Constantine's son.

With a population of over 100,000 in the 6th century, Constantinople was at the height of its glory, even as the once proud Aegean coastal cities sank into oblivion as little more than fishing villages. The empire's wealth invited attack by Avars from central Asia, Slavs, Persians and Arabs. While Byzantine possessions around the Mediterranean fell to the new Islamic empire, Constantinople stood firm. In the 8th and 9th centuries, a theological dispute raged within the Orthodox Church over the use of "graven images", in the course of which thousands of statues and icons were destroyed in Byzantine churches.

Turks and Crusaders

The Selçuk Turks, nomads from Central Asia, entered the Byzantine realm in the 11th century. Converting to Islam as mercenary soldiers for the Abbasid Arab empire, they gradually took control of the territories they conquered in the Middle East. The Selçuks drove the Byzantines

from Anatolia and established their capital at Konya in 1099.

Retrenched at the European extremity of the Byzantine Empire, Constantinople still possessed great wealth and prestige, prompting merchants from Venice, Pisa, Amalfi and Genoa to set up shop. In exchange for generous trading privileges, the emperors sought the help of the Europeans to reconquer lands lost to the Turks. The rape, massacre and plunder wrought by four Crusades from 1096 to 1204 did more harm to this beleaguered outpost of Christianity than to the Islamic foe. In each case, European armies had to be bought off with paid shipment to Asia Minor and booty from lands conquered on their mission to "save" Jerusalem from the infidel.

Led by the Venetians, the Fourth Crusade (1202–04) got embroiled in inimitable Byzantine palace intrigues among rival pretenders to the throne. The knightly champions of Christianity burned, pillaged and raped their way through Constantinople, ousted the Greek Byzantine claimants and installed their own man, the Count of Flanders, on the throne as Baldwin I, Emperor of Constantinople. The Latin Empire lasted 57 years, under constant assault from Bulgars and Turks, while the Greeks regrouped to the east in a Byzantine government-in-exile at Nicaea (Iznik). Their leader Michael Palaeologus (1261–82) profited from conflict among Venetian and Genoese merchants to reconquer Constantinople.

Final Conquest

Meanwhile, a new wave of invaders left the Selçuk empire in ruins, and a tougher breed of Turks emerged to take over Anatolia by 1290. The dynasty that lasted over six centuries was founded in 1299 by Osman I—"Ottoman" to the western world. As they closed in on Constantinople, the Ottomans showed considerable religious tolerance towards the Christians whose lands they seized. After 1330, Osman's son Orhan set up his capital across the Marmara sea at Bursa, took Nicaea and married the daughter of Byzantine emperor John VI. Thrace, north of Constantinople, fell to Orhan's son, Murad I. His men, too, married into the Byzantine nobility to gain military support against the Slavs and Hungarians.

In 1402, Tamerlane's Mongol invasion of Anatolia gave the Byzantine Empire a 50-year respite. Sultan Mehmet II triumphed in Ottoman palace intrigues to prepare the final assault on Constantinople. When the Turkish siege began in April, 1453, the town's population had dwindled to 35,000. In response to a request from the last emperor, Constantine XI, for help from Europe, 700 mercenaries were sent from Genoa, under Giovanni Giustiniani. With their siege machines and wily tactics, the huge Turkish army made short work of the massive reinforced ramparts and great chain stretched across the Golden Horn to stop enemy ships. The emperor died in battle, and Sultan Mehmet turned the church of St Sophia into a mosque.

Ottoman Empire

Even-handed in their religious tolerance, the first Ottoman rulers invited Italian, French and Greek communities back to Constantinople, as well as thousands of Jews expelled from Spain in 1492. The Turks referred to the city as Istanbul, a name adopted abroad only in the 20th century.

Ottoman power reached its height under Suleiman the Magnificent (1520–66), great lawgiver and builder of both empire and of monuments. A distinctive Turkish architectural style was originated by his master architect, Sinan, who by his own estimate designed 334 mosques, schools, hospitals, public baths, bridges and palaces. To control trade routes to Egypt, Suleiman seized the island of Rhodes and 13 the port of Bodrum. The western Mediterranean was "managed" for him by the pirate Barbarossa, whom he made admiral of the Ottoman fleet. Expansion across Hungary was stopped only at the walls of Vienna in 1529. At home, he negotiated "capitulations" exempting French residents from Ottoman taxes and court jurisdiction (privileges that were later extended to other foreign residents as Turkish power declined). Suleiman's court continued the old Byzantine capital's time-honoured tradition of palace intrigue. The machinations of his concubines and their sons heralded the long process of decadence.

Over the next three centuries, while Europe was being reinvigorated by the Renaissance, exploration of the Americas and Asia and the Industrial Revolution, Turkey rested on its laurels. A corps of headstrong Janissary soldiers (Yeniçeri), originally Christian prisoners of war converted to Islam, took care of internal stability—and frequently fomented conflict. At the end of the 18th century, spurred by ripples from the French Revolution, Ottoman reforms were aborted by a revolt of conservative forces allied to the Janissaries. In 1826 the latter were finally crushed by the sultan's more loyal Spahi cavalry.

Atatürk's Republic

The 19th-century modernization—secular schools, newspapers, Westernized clothes, European-style diplomacy and civil service—came too late. Indeed, constitutional change and the end of the empire were hastened by the first politically aware graduates of the new schools forming the nationalistic Society of Young Ottomans, followed by army officers, lawyers and teachers known as Young Turks. After a revolt at Thessaloniki (Salonica) in 1908, the Young Turks overcame conservative opposition to a new parliament and replaced Sultan Abdül Al-Hamid II with his younger brother Mehmet V. The rebels' political wing, Committee for Union and Progress (CUP), imposed authoritarian government, siding with Germany in World War I.

Turkey became a republic in 1923, moving its capital to Ankara and making Mustafa Kemal its first president. Better known by his adopted name of Atatürk (Father of the Turks), the brilliant but despotic architect of the new nation rose to prominence with Turkey's single military triumph of World War I, halting the Allies at Gallipoli in 1915. After defeating the Greeks in the wars of 1919–22, he headed the Turkish National

Assembly which abolished the sultanate. From 1925 to 1935, Atatürk's drastic reforms force-marched Turkey into the modern age. Agriculture, industry and the legal system were all remodelled on Western lines. Islamic authority was replaced by secular institutions, the alphabet of the Turkish language was changed almost overnight from Arabic to Latin, women were given the vote in 1934, and the traditional fez and turban were banned in towns. At his death in 1938, Atatürk was revered nationwide, but strangely not beloved.

Into the Future

Intimidated by Nazi Germany into World War II neutrality, the modern Turkish state benefited from massive US aid in 1946 and remained solidly anchored to the west in the post-war era. Parliamentary government has alternated with military dictatorship as the country grapples with industrial and agricultural reforms.

In recent years, Turkey has been trying to reconcile two goals of its dual Asian and European identity: a strong alliance with the group of Turkic-speaking republics emerging from the former Soviet Union, and entry to the European Union. After electing its first woman prime minister, Tansu Çiller, in 1993, the country seemed determined to maintain a forward-looking stance. But the 1996 electoral success of the Islamicist Refah (Welfare) party produced a fragile—and short-lived—coalition of religious and secular forces. Their successors, the pro-Islamic AKP, face the delicate task of asserting Turkey's Islamic traditions while Atatürk's portrait remains in shops and offices as a symbol of the modern age.

TWO SUPERB CRUISES One of the particular joys of Istanbul's situation on the waterways is the boat-cruises you can take from the Eminönü docks near the Galata Bridge. Sailing the **Bosphorus** past its country mansions and fishing villages to the Black Sea, whether it be in a private vessel or public water-bus, is romantic through and through. Another day-trip, out to the **Princes' Islands** in the Sea of Marmara, gives you a charming view of where the well-heeled citizens of Istanbul relax in their week-end and summer villas.

15

On the Scene

We have divided Turkey's sprawling metropolis into three sections: historic Old Istanbul on the European shore, modern Istanbul across the Golden Horn inlet and the Asian shore's Üsküdar district. From Istanbul you can cross the Bosphorus to Anatolia's west coast, or head for Ankara and its fascinating hinterland.

▶ ISTANBUL
Old Istanbul, Modern Istanbul, Asian Shore

From your first sight of the graceful minarets and domes, factory chimneys and skyscrapers of Istanbul's skyline, it is clear that this is a town where Asia and Europe live inseparably side by side. When you start out on your first walk it becomes even more apparent. That bright young man in a business suit, muttering so intently into his mobile phone, nearly bumps into the old tea-vendor in traditional headgear and tunic, offering glasses of his steaming amber brew from a spouted brass urn hanging from his shoulders. You will sense this rich fusion of cultures wherever you wander,

More than 21,000 ceramic tiles cover the interior walls of the Blue Mosque.

among the palaces and bazaars, mosques and churches of Old Istanbul, or the boutiques, nightclubs, restaurants, cafés—and Internet cafés—of the modern city.

Linked by bridges, each of the three districts—old, modern and Asian—is surrounded by two of the city's three stretches of water. Old Istanbul has the Sea of Marmara along its south shore, and to the north the Golden Horn inlet separates it from the modern city. The Bosphorus channel divides the modern city from the Asian shore, which in turn continues along the Sea of Marmara.

As you amble around, just beware of two risks to life and limb: pedestrians have no priority over the cars and trams that hurtle along at breakneck speed; and even the pavement, with its

Over the door of St Sophia, Constantine presents a model of the city and Justinian a model of the church to the Virgin and Child.

steep kerbs, potholes and sudden steps up and down, is not a totally safe haven.

Old Istanbul

The ancient heart of the city, now known as Sultanahmet district, takes its name from the Sultan Ahmet Mosque—also called the Blue Mosque. The district also includes monuments from the time of Emperor Constantine, Justinian's great church of St Sophia and the Ottoman palace of Topkapı. With its other palaces, museums and above all the Grand Bazaar, the Old City is the natural place to begin any tour of Istanbul.

St Sophia (Ayasofya)

Despite the four minarets flanking the edifice, *Hagia Sophia* (Divine Wisdom), as it is known to Greek Orthodoxy, has been restored to its original status of a basilica, though it functions now only as a museum. Emperor Justinian completed this greatest monument of the Orthodox Church in 537, five years after an earlier basilica built by Constantine the Great had burned to the ground during a bloody revolt. From the outside, the much reconstructed sprawling block may now seem decidedly unprepossessing, but the awesome interior of the domed rectangle makes clear its inspiration to architects throughout the Christian and Islamic world. Most of its golden treasures were plundered—not by the conquering Turks, who converted the basilica into a mosque, but by Christian Crusaders 350 years earlier.

Over the vast, square central hall soars the great cupola 31 m (101 ft) in diameter and 55 m (180 ft) high, supported on massive arched piers. In the vestibule, narthex entrance-hall, apse and galleries surrounding the nave, there are splendid mosaics of Mary, Jesus, the archangels and various Byzantine emperors and empresses, dating for the most part back to the 12th century. From its 500 years as a mosque remain the prayer-niche (*mihrab*) in the apse, the pulpit (*mimber*), the sultan's loggia and the Arabic-inscribed medallions.

Hippodrome

Southwest of St Sophia, the chariots have been replaced by buses and taxis and the marble grandstands recycled to build the Blue Mosque, but the grass-covered shape of the ancient Roman hippodrome is still there. Its arena seated over 100,000 spectators for both sporting and political events. In 330, Constantine the Great presided here over ceremonies founding his new capital. Between chariot races, agitators harangued the fans to protest against the Byzantine emperors' religious or social policies.

Today an imposing domed fountain, offered by Germany's Kaiser Wilhelm II on a state visit in 1898, stands at the arena's northern end. Towards the other end are three older monuments. The hieroglyphics on the upper section of the Egyptian obelisk

HOOLIGANS ANCIENT AND MODERN

Istanbul's formidable football supporters, particularly those of the town's most famous team, Galatasaray, are notorious throughout Europe. But they are gentle as lambs compared to sports fans in Byzantine times. Chariot races at the Hippodrome were only a pretext for coming together to stir up riots over heavy taxes or abuse of religious icons. Divided into proletarian Greens and more aristocratic Blues, the fans arrived with rocks and daggers concealed in their picnic baskets. Their victims often numbered in the hundreds. At the games of 532, Emperor Justinian's "conciliatory" speech at the end of the 22nd race so enraged both Greens and Blues that they joined forces, stormed out into the streets of Constantinople and set fire to the whole city.

19

show that it was built for the pharaoh Thutmosis III in the 15th century BC, while the base depicts how it was shipped to Constantinople for Emperor Theodosius in AD 390. On a truncated serpentine column brought by Constantine from Delphi, three bronze serpents originally supporting a golden vase celebrate a Greek victory over the Persians in 479 BC. Of the ancient obelisk restored by Constantine Porphyrogenitus, a Byzantine emperor of the 10th century, there's nothing to see but sorry-looking stone remains.

Blue Mosque (Sultanahmet Camii)

Built in 1616 by Sultan Ahmet, the imposing mosque is for some an inspired masterpiece, and for others a defiant architectural statement of Ottoman decadence. Despite its undeniably graceful silhouette, it brings nothing new to the variations Islamic architects had wrought on the St Sophia model across the Hippodrome. And holy men were shocked by the apparently sacrilegious challenge which its six minarets appeared to make to the six of the mosque at Mecca—four being otherwise the norm. Like St Sophia, the structure's full beauty is in the interior, where over 20,000 blue Iznik ceramic tiles impart an ethereal light to the vast hall of worship. Standing behind the visitors' wooden railing, you'll find that a pair of binoculars is useful to appreciate the ornate white marble pulpit and the prayer-niche set in the wall facing Mecca.

Basilica Cistern

Northwest of the Hippodrome, a marvel of excavation and restoration has been performed to reveal ancient underground cisterns, probably providing water for Constantine's capital since the 4th century. This eerily beautiful forest of granite pillars, many with fine Corinthian capitals, and brick vaults in a herringbone pattern is erroneously but understandably also known as the Sunken Palace (Yerebatan Sarayı). Music and subdued lighting accompany you on a mysterious tour along boardwalks over some 80,000 cubic metres of water. In a far corner, seek out two huge sculpted Medusa heads sunken in the water, one inverted and the other on its side, stoically supporting two of the sturdy pillars.

Topkapı Palace

After its foundation by Mehmet the Conqueror in 1459, Topkapı (which literally means Cannon Gate) remained the seat of Ottoman power for four centuries. This is no mere palace.

With tree-shaded gardens extending over to the Bosphorus, it grew into a veritable town-within-a-town of royal apartments, bath houses, schools, libraries, mosques, council halls, courts of justice, guardrooms, treasury and mint. A wander round the four courtyards today will give you a concentrated sense of the vast enterprise that was the Ottoman Empire—and of its style, both in the brutal wielding of power and the seductive taste for luxury.

Beyond a graceful 18th-century fountain and Mehmet's great imperial gate, Bab-ı-Hümayün, lies the first, outer courtyard. The visitors disembarking from taxis and buses recapture the bustle of throngs gathering here to serve or petition the sultan. The Byzantine church of St Irene in this shady courtyard, used

A sultan's view from Topkapı's marble terrace.

as a storehouse in Ottoman times, is closed to the public except for concerts during the Istanbul Festival in June.

From the Middle Gate *(Orta Kapı)* ticket-office, the second courtyard fans out into gardens of rose bushes, cypresses and plane trees. To the right, a row of domes and monumental chimneys (built by Suleiman the Magnificent's master architect Mimar Sinan) tops the ten splendid palace kitchens. They once employed 1,500 cooks and servants, and now house the sultans' collection of porcelain. You can also see an astonishing battery of utensils in the area where confectioners made *loukoum* and other Turkish delights.

On the west side of the courtyard, old accounting offices now display a fearsome collection of weapons and armour. Next door are the Divan chambers, with a couch along three sides of the room. The Divan was the State Council, presided by the Grand Vizier. You can see an inner iron-grill window, the "Eye of the Sultan" through which he watched the goings-on.

In the corner of the courtyard behind the Divan is the entrance to the Harem. For a separate fee you can take a lightning guided tour of some of the 400 rooms that make up the quarters of the sultan's wives and concubines. From the Arabic *harim,* "forbidden", the off-limits area was reserved for the women who attended to the ruler's pleasure and assured him of at least one male heir. Their numbers rose to 809 under the 19th-century Sultan Abdülaziz.

As barrack rooms flanking the entrance attest, the women were guarded in the daytime by halberdiers, who wore blinkers when entering the residential quarters, and at night by black eunuchs, who were thought not to need blinkers. Running the day-to-day activities was the domain of the often omnipotent mother of the sultan, who conveniently located her opulent residence between the rooms of the wives and concubines and the grandiose apartments of the sultan. Highlights are the 16th-century bedroom of Murat III with its indoor swimming pool, the grand Imperial Hall *(Hünkar Sofası)*, a 17th-century library, and the tiles and painted wooden panels of Ahmet III's charmingly rococo dining room.

In the third courtyard, visit the Palace Treasury, a stupendous display of decadent extravagance. Besides a great emerald-encrusted dagger in its gold and diamond sheath (for which Peter Ustinov was nearly killed in the *Topkapi* movie caper), see the Spoonmaker's Diamond, an 86-carat bauble set amid 49 other priceless sparklers.

Like the sultans, take tea in the fourth courtyard, which contains several pavilions and terraces, a restaurant and café. Next to Bagdat Pavilion, built for Murat IV, is the small gilt-roofed Iftariye Baldachin, where the sultan could sit in the shade and admire the views of the Bosphorus and Golden Horn.

Museum of Turkish and Islamic Art

On the west side of the Hippodrome, across from the Blue Mosque, the handsome palace of Ibrahim Paşa provides an appropriate setting for these art collections. The home of Suleiman the Magnificent's grand vizier was built in 1524 and reconstructed to the original design in the 19th century. In subtly lit rooms round a central garden courtyard, exquisite carpets and kilims, ceramics, jewellery and traditional artefacts display the country's rich culture of the Selçuk, Mameluke and Ottoman eras.

Archaeology Museum

To the west of of Topkapı Palace, in the first courtyard, the museum has a compact collection of Greco-Roman art, notably sculpted sarcophagi from the 4th century BC. The Alexander Sarcophagus, decorated with battle scenes of Alexander the Great, is the prize exhibit. On an upper floor is a fine display of ancient Anatolian art, with jewellery from Troy.

Museum of the Ancient Orient

Next door, this museum displays such finds as Hittite stone lions and Babylonian ceramic panels. Don't miss the Tiled Pavilion from 1472 in the courtyard, from which the sultan would watch polo games. Today it is a showplace for a superb collection of Iznik tiles, plates and vases.

Burnt Column

From Sultanahmet district, the easiest route to the Grand Bazaar takes you along the bustling Divan Yolu thoroughfare past Constantine's Burnt Column—in Turkish it's called Çemberlitaş,

or "hooped stone", referring to the bands of iron used to hold it together after an earthquake. It was said to have contained in its base nails from the Crucifixion and pieces of the Cross brought here by the emperor's mother, Helen. The Çemberlitaş Hamam, nearby, is a venerable Turkish bath founded in the 16th century by Nur Banu, the all-powerful Mother of the Sultan.

Grand Bazaar

Like Topkapı, the Grand Bazaar (Kapali Çarşi) is a town all to itself, founded in 1461 and rebuilt many times since. In the maze of dome-covered streets, alleys and squares, you'll find small mosques, fountains, restaurants, cafés, banks, a post office and a police station, in addition to some 4,000 shops. Carpets, ceramics, leatherware, fabrics and jewellery—delightful treasures and hallucinating junk—are offered with the same gentle smile, glass of tea and charming sales talk. At the Sandal Bedesten market square, auctions are held at lunchtime on Tuesday (furniture), Wednesday (carpets) and Thursday (jewellery).

Don't try to find your way around the bazaar with a map, it's much more satisfying to get gloriously lost. To find your way out, as in a forest, just keep going straight ahead.

23

Mosque of Suleiman the Magnificent

Up on its terrace to the north of Istanbul University, the mosque, with its magnificently orchestrated cluster of domes and minarets, dominates the horizon of the Golden Horn. The mosque is the centrepiece of the vast Süleymaniye complex, embracing library, schools, bath houses, caravanserai hostelry and monumental tombs. Built in 1557 for the most powerful of Ottoman sultans, it is regarded by many as the greatest achievement of Suleiman's architect, Mimar Sinan.

Columns of porphyry, marble and pink Egyptian granite form the portico of the grand rectangular forecourt. Through tall doors inlaid with ivory, mother-of-pearl and ebony, you will discover the mosque's luminous interior beneath a dome 53 m (173 ft) high and 26.5 m (87 ft) in diameter. It is lit by 200 windows, 32 set in the dome itself.

In the cemetery at the rear of the mosque, Suleiman's monumental tomb is topped by the sultan's great turban beneath a dome of gold, red and black glittering with ceramic stars. Next door is the tomb of his favourite wife, Roxelana. Rare privilege for a commoner, the architect's tomb is housed in a triangular garden with octagonal fountain at the northeast corner of the Süleymaniye complex.

Eminönü

The district between the Grand Bazaar and the boats moored by Galata Bridge teems with craftsmen and vendors conducting their affairs in a labyrinth of narrow streets and often steeply sloping back alleys. Eminönü is noisy, aromatic and full of colour, a great place in which to forget your camera and just look, smell and listen. Parked in front of Sirkeci railway station is one of the old steam engines that brought the Orient Express here to its Istanbul terminus.

Besides being a major artery to the modern city, Galata Bridge is

THREE LUXURIOUS PALACES The Ottoman sultans often had more money than taste, but their palaces bear eloquent testimony to their flair for the good life: the labyrinthine **Topkapı** in the old city and two spectacular residences on the Bosphorus, **Dolmabahçe** and, appropriately transformed into a luxury hotel, the **Çirağan**.

the starting-point for the Bosphorus ferry-service.

Spice Market

The big, clumsy Yeni Mosque towering over the Golden Horn attracts more beggars than architectural buffs. But behind it is the wonderful Spice Market, also known as Egyptian Bazaar *(Mısır Çarşısı)* since it collected customs duty on goods coming in from Cairo. Many a *bon vivant* prefers this place to the Grand Bazaar. Not only will you find every imaginable spice and herb, culinary, aphrodisiac or rejuvenating, but the best sweetmeats—Turkish delight *(loukoum)* and hazelnut or pistachio-flavoured *helva*. Flowers, exotic love-birds and parrots grace the open section of the market.

Rüstem Paşa Mosque

In a back street west of the market is a charming smaller mosque, the Rüstem Paşa, built for Suleiman's grand vizier and son-in-law. It is noted for its brilliantly coloured Iznik tiles decorated with tulips and carnations.

Golden Horn

Horn-shaped, OK, but golden? The smelly inlet's name comes from the Greek *Chrysokeras,* with the not very serious explanation that the Byzantines sank their gold and jewellery in it during the Turkish siege of 1453. You won't find many treasure-hunters prepared to dive into the polluted waters to check out the legend. (The Turkish name *Haliç* just means "estuary".) It can be navigated on a casual ferry-service from Galata Bridge.

Neighbourhoods to the west along the Old Istanbul shore of the inlet were once enclaves for the Greeks and Jews. In the Fener district, home of the Greek Orthodox Patriarchate, a few churches and high school continue to serve the tiny Greek community. The Balat quarter still has its synagogues and Jewish cemetery, long after its Jews crossed the Golden Horn to join their more prosperous cousins in the modern city; the majority subsequently moved on to Israel. The town's oldest synagogue, Ahrida, was recently restored for the 500th anniversary of the arrival of the first Jews in 1492, after their expulsion from Spain.

At the inlet's western tip is the revered pilgrimage mosque of Eyüp, beautiful burial place of Mohammed's standard-bearer and a popular cemetery for devout Muslims. Important shipyards are active across the inlet at Hasköy.

Aqueduct of Valens

In a pleasant park west of the Süleymaniye, the Aqueduct of 25

Valens stands proudly 18.5 m (60 ft) over Atatürk boulevard, 1,600 years after the ruler of the Eastern Empire built it. Until the late 19th century, frequently restored, it continued to bring water from the reservoirs of the Belgrade Forest up the European shore of the Bosphorus. This segment of the handsome double-tiered structure extends 800 m (2,624 ft) in the direction of the royal palaces it used to serve.

Kariye Camii

Another historic monument worth a trip beyond the old city centre is the Church of St Saviour in Chora, out near the ramparts. This Byzantine treasure, in a pretty setting of traditional wooden houses, is now preserved as a museum for its beautifully restored cycles of mosaics and frescoes. The works devoted to the lives of Mary and Jesus were created in the 14th century, some 200 years after the church's construction. The most celebrated of the frescoes, depicting the Resurrection, are in the pareecclesion, or burial chapel, to the right of the nave.

Kumkapı District

Along the Marmara shore, the Kumkapı district is a magnet at night time for its seafood restaurants, but it's really worth a daytime visit, too, to see the strikingly attractive display of the catch at its fish market.

Byzantine Ramparts

The Theodosian Walls which defended Constantinople from landward attack from the west were completed in 413 and have been restored many times since. The walls now provide shelter

---

MIMAR SINAN, ROYAL ARCHITECT (1489–1588)

The master builder of Suleiman the Magnificent's finest monuments—and many for his successors Selim II and Murat III—was born of a Christian family, though it is not known whether they were Armenian, Greek, Croatian or Albanian. When he became a member of the Janissary corps, he converted to Islam, and it was on military service in Egypt, Persia, Serbia and Greece that he acquired his breadth of architectural knowledge. His work as a military engineer of fortifications, harbours and bridges prompted Suleiman in 1539 to make him court architect for his mosques, palaces and tombs. In those days when sultans gave you more than a ticking off if you earned their displeasure, it was a tribute to Sinan's skill and diplomacy that he served three of them and died in his bed aged 99.

for gypsy encampments, surrounded by chickens, horses and sheep. The best places to see the impressive structure are at Yedikule at the southern end near the Sea of Marmara, or north at Edirnekapı, combined with a visit to the nearby Church of St Saviour.

Extending 6.6 km (4 miles) from the Sea of Marmara to the Golden Horn, the whole fortification system originally comprised an inner wall, an outer wall and a moat, with dozens of bastions along the way. At Yedikule ("seven towers", four of them Byzantine and three Turkish), the fortifications surround the Golden Gate (now bricked up) which served as a triumphal arch for Byzantine emperors. Though Yedikule looks like a castle, it was never a residence—except for the state's political enemies shut up in the two prison towers.

At Edirnekapı is the Adrianople Gate through which Mehmet the Conqueror rode in 1453 —after his cannon had left this part of the walls in their present eloquent state of ruin.

Modern Istanbul

The Galata district on the north shore of the Golden Horn has always had a more cosmopolitan atmosphere than Old Istanbul. This reached its height in the 18th and 19th centuries, when the European powers built their elegant neoclassical embassies here. They continued doing business as consulates after Atatürk moved the modern capital to Ankara.

In the Middle Ages, Galata was set aside for the city's foreign merchants, Genoese and Venetian in the main, joined by Jews expelled from Spain in the 16th century, then by refugees from Greece and Armenia—and at all times by a rowdy bunch of itinerant seamen and prostitutes.

The large foreign contingents have gone, and only a small Jewish community remains. But Beyoğlu, the smarter quarter of the Galata district, has retained the old mixture of European sophistication and, around the edges, the seedy rumbustiousness of any great sea port. (Galata takes its name from the Gallic tribe settling here in 279 BC.)

Galata Tower

The landmark of the modern city was built by the Genoese in 1349, now 68 m (223 ft) high but originally much taller until 1453, when the two upper levels of what was then called the Tower of Christ were lopped off by the Turks. On May 29 of that year, as an inscription on the wall notes, Sultan Mehmet received from the Genoese the keys to the

Galata colony. From the rooftop restaurant, the panoramic views over the Bosphorus and Golden Horn are magnificent, especially in the evening.

Pera Palace Hotel

Another landmark, on Meşrutiyet Caddesi, this is one of those legendary hotels to be compared with the New York Plaza, the London Savoy or the Paris Ritz. See it not for its luxury—somewhat faded since its heyday when built in 1892 for passengers of the Orient Express—but for the elegant memories of the lobby with its handsome Art Deco elevator, a splendid old bar, and the intimate alcoves of a teashop whose pastry and Turkish delight are still the toast of Istanbul. Room 101, where Atatürk slept, has been preserved as a museum in which you can see some of his personal possessions displayed in glass cases, such as monogrammed underwear, his knife and fork, toothbrush and tooth powder, and binoculars.

Istiklâl Caddesi

Beyoğlu's main thoroughfare begins at the terminus of the Tünel underground railway, built by the French at the turn of the century, less than a kilometre uphill from the north end of Galata Bridge. Apart from the embassies turned consulates, the Europeans also built their churches here: the Franciscans' Roman Catholic church of St Antoine, the Dutch Protestant Union Church and the Greek Orthodox Aghia Triada. They are surrounded now by fashionable boutiques, cinemas and garish nightclubs. Apart from a tramway, the boulevard has been

4

FOUR GREAT BYZANTINE MONUMENTS

The tolerant and above all pragmatic Ottomans did not systematically destroy all traces of their predecessors. In Istanbul, the **Church of St Sophia** has inspired the best of the city's mosques. Superb 14th-century mosaics and frescoes can be seen in the **Church of St Saviour**. The **Byzantine Ramparts**—with a few Turkish additions—still enclose the western periphery of the Old City. Oldest of all, Constantine's **Basilica Cistern** has been unearthed to reveal all the splendour of a subterranean palace.

transformed into a pedestrian zone. The side streets are full of bars, cafés, colourful restaurants, the best known being the old artists' haunts on Çiçek Pasajı (Flower Passage).

Just off Galatasaray Square is the handsome entrance to the French *lycée* of the same name, a prestigious school better known outside Istanbul for the football team founded from its sports club.

Taksim Square

This vast bustling space at the north end of Istiklâl Caddesi is a boisterous assertion of Turkish modernity. Traffic hurtles round its office blocks and supremely functional hotels at breakneck speed. The only respite is in the Atatürk Cultural Centre, on the east side of the square, headquarters in summer of the city's international arts festival.

Military Museum

North of Taksim Square on Cumhuriyet Caddesi, this museum is less interesting for the relics of Ottoman military exploits than for the rousing afternoon concerts of the Janissary marching band—usually Wednesday to Sunday at 3 p.m. The fierce Janissary troops were disbanded in 1826 but their Mehter Band was reinstated in 1914. What Scottish bagpipes did for the British, Janissary musicians did for the Turks, striking the fear of Allah into the hearts of their enemies ever since the 14th century.

Dolmabahçe Palace

Istanbul's transition to a modern city began with this sprawling latterday Versailles, monumental last gasp of the Ottoman Empire. It was from here, on the European shore of the Bosphorus, that Mehmet the Conqueror launched his final assault on Constantinople and that the last, deposed sultan left ignominiously in a British warship five centuries later.

In the 1840s, feeling threatened by growing rumbles of revolt outside the walls of Topkapı, Sultan Abdülmecit I sought a safer home on the city outskirts. The visitor can only be dumbfounded that with an empire hopelessly in debt, the sultan had held onto enough of a private fortune to build himself a vast gleaming white marble edifice and fill it with Gobelin tapestries, every imaginable style of western and Oriental furniture, Sèvres porcelain, dozens of chandeliers (the biggest was a gift from Queen Victoria) and other monstrous baubles of Baccarat, Bohemian and Irish crystal—even the balustrade of the ceremonial double staircase is made of crystal.

29

Atatürk turned the place into a public museum, and a high point for tour-guides is the modest apartment where the great leader died on November 10, 1938, at 9.05 a.m., the time at which all the palace clocks have been stopped.

Asian Shore

Reached by ferry from the Eminönü jetty, the blessedly peaceful district of Üsküdar enjoys an intriguing coexistence between Islamic traditionalists and a growing colony of avant-garde artists and writers. After the noise of European Istanbul, it is a pleasure just to wander around the narrow winding lanes of old wooden balconied houses, cafés, studios and galleries.

Mihrimah Mosque

Up on a terrace right by the ferry landing, Mihrimah Mosque is an early work of Mimar Sinan built in 1548 for Suleiman the Magnificent's daughter. Its cluster of three half-domes around the central cupola seems to prop it up against the hillside behind.

Yeni Valide Mosque

Across the broad Iskele Square is the 18th-century mosque built by Ahmet III for his mother and enhanced by her monumental tomb and a fine fountain for the worshippers' ritual ablutions.

Two Markets

The food market is scattered in side streets leading off Iskele Square, with a remarkably rich variety of fruit and vegetables brought in from the Anatolian farms.

South of the square, along Büyük Hamam Street, the Üsküdar Flea Market has, besides its second-hand furniture, a good array of jewellery, wood carving, brassware and other ornaments.

Büyük Çamlıca

About 6 km (4 miles) northeast of Üsküdar, this hill, 268 m (879 ft), gives you a grand view over old and new Istanbul, the Bosphorus and Sea of Marmara.

Florence Nightingale Museum

The district known as Scutari to 19th-century Europeans served as a British military base in the Crimean War (1854–56). Florence Nightingale ran the army hospital, now part of the Selimiye Barracks on the southern edge of town and converted to a museum of the nurse's personal belongings and books. The nearby British War Cemetery contains graves from the Crimean and the two world wars.

Along the Bosphorus shores, the ornate wooden houses almost get their toes wet.

With an early start, each of these excursions can be managed in a day trip, though you may find that Bursa or Gallipoli merit an overnight stay. The Gallipoli trip is often combined with a tour of that other famous battlefield across the Dardanelles at Troy. The boat cruises to Princes' Islands and up the Bosphorus both start out from the Eminönü side of Galata Bridge.

Princes' Islands

Of the nine islands out in the Sea of Marmara, four are inhabited as holiday resorts for the Istanbul bourgeoisie. After a pleasant ferry trip from Sirkeci Pier, you can tour the islands in horse-drawn carriages, on a donkey or on a rented bicycle. Surrounded by pine forests and gardens of bougainvillaea and wisteria, elegant old villas and cottages enjoy a tranquillity free of motor traffic. The princely name dates back to the time when the Byzantine emperors used the islands as gilded cages for their family enemies.

Büyükada, the biggest and now most popular island, was for four years the home of Bolshevik leader Leon Trotsky after he was expelled from Russia by Joseph Stalin in 1929. The old revolutionary took time off from writing bitter tracts denouncing his arch-enemy to fish for mackerel and lobster. The restaurants down by the ferry landing still offer some good, but expensive seafood. The monasteries on the island's two hills were founded in the Middle Ages and occasionally served as asylums for the insane.

On neighbouring Heybeliada, the lovely beaches attract water sports enthusiasts, while ramblers head for the pine woods. The smaller Burgaz and Kınalı islands are remoter retreats for hermits and artists.

The Bosphorus

A trip by public ferry or private charter along the channel linking the Black Sea and Sea of Marmara is a highlight of any visit to Turkey. As the boat cruises along the Galata coast, you start with a whole new perspective on monuments you may have already visited on land—the Dolmabahçe Palace and, newly renovated as a luxury hotel since a devastating fire in 1910, the Çirağan Palace built by Sultan Abdülaziz in 1874. Between the two is a monument to Barbarossa, the 16th-century pirate extraordinary promoted to admiral of the Ottoman

The quayside near 19th-century Ortaköy Mosque is a favourite meeting place for families and courting couples.

fleet. The hill behind is covered with the woods of Yıldız Park.

You will pass a succession of wooden waterfront villas called *yalıs,* both grand and dilapidated, fishing villages, seafood restaurants, consulates and palaces. In the shadow of the first arching Bosphorus Bridge, on the European shore opposite Beylerbeyi Palace, is Ortaköy's delightful neo-baroque mosque.

Beyond the bridge, prosperous Istanbul families have residences in Arnavutköy, an old Albanian settlement, and Bebek.

Further up this European shore, Rumeli Hisarı is the fortress built by Mehmet in 1452 to prepare his assault on Constantinople. Across the straits are the remains of the Ottomans' earlier castle, Anadolu Hisarı.

The fishing villages most popular for their seafood restaurants are Tarabya, Sarıyer and Rumeli Kavağı on the European shore, and the cheaper Anadolu Kavağı over on the Asian side. This is the terminus for the public ferry. Climb up to the hilltop Byzantine castle ruin for a magnificent view over the Black Sea and back down the Bosphorus.

Bursa

Inland from the Sea of Marmara's industrialized south coast, Bursa 33 is attractively set in a fertile poplar-lined plain of fruit and nut orchards. Behind it, olive groves cover the lower slopes of Uludağ, the "great mountain" rising to 2,543 m (8,344 ft). The town prospers from its silk and textile industries and owes its animated atmosphere to an active university community. In the ancient citadel are the tombs of Osman Gazi, founder of the Ottoman dynasty, and his son Orhan, dating back to the 14th century when Bursa was the empire's first capital.

Heading east, you can stroll through the street market, its stalls piled high with the region's produce. The covered bazaar is popular for its locally manufactured silks and other fabrics.

Among the town's many notable mosques is the 14th-century 20-domed Ulu Cami (Great Mosque), with a pretty fountain protected by a cupola. The splendid 15th-century Yeşil Cami (Green Mosque) has a superb tiled interior; Mehmet I made it his headquarters and took up residence in a suite above the main entrence. He is buried behind the mosque, on the other side of the street, in the turquoise-tiled Yeşil Turbe (Green Mausoleum).

The Museum of Turkish and Islamic Art is attractively housed in the Green Mosque's old theology school. Around the Muradiye Mosque complex, look out for the Ottoman houses. In Koza Park, you may catch a Karagöz puppet show with its cheeky clowns, a genre which originated in Bursa.

Gallipoli

Commanding access from the Mediterranean to Marmara and the Black Sea beyond, the Dardanelles strait has been a bone of contention throughout history, from the time of Homer's Troy to Atatürk's Gallipoli (Gelibolu). The battlefields and Allied cemeteries of World War I are strung out along the picturesque pine-covered peninsula. With Turkey on the German side in 1915, this region became the target of a two-pronged attack by Anglo-French forces to the south and Australian-New Zealand (ANZAC) troops to the north. Pinned down by the Turks, the Allies found that what was planned as a lightning assault turned into disastrous trench-warfare costing both sides a total of over 100,000 dead. Casualties were particularly heavy for the Australians and New Zealanders. Cemeteries and assault beaches are eloquently signposted Shell Green, Shrapnel Valley and Anzac Cove. On Çonkbayırı Hill is the New Zealanders' memorial obelisk and a Turkish monument celebrating the deeds and words of field commander Mustafa Kemal, the future Atatürk.

▶ WEST COAST
Troy, Pergamum, Izmir, Kuşadası, Ephesus,
Three Ionian Cities, Pamukkale, Bodrum, Marmaris

Visitors to Anatolia's west coast can combine the hedonistic delights of its beach resorts with the stimulation of fascinating archaeological sites. The Aegean coast from the Dardanelles strait to Bodrum was the site of some of ancient Greece's most prosperous colonies. The monuments they left are practically all within easy reach for day trips from one or other of the major resorts.

Troy
The setting of Homer's epic *Iliad* has been uncovered on an inland hill near the entrance to the Dardanelles. Any lover of history or legend will want to make the pilgrimage. On the main highway 25 km (15 miles) south of the port city of Çanakkale, signposts point west to Troy (Truva). This is the place where Sparta's beautiful Queen Helen was kept in Priam's royal palace, and where Odysseus sent in an armoured personnel carrier disguised as a wooden horse. Here are remains of the walls around which Achilles dragged the body of his heroic enemy, Hector.

The legends are commonly regarded as a splendid embellishment of actual deeds of piracy and war carried out by Greek ships on the Anatolian coast in the 13th century BC. Whether the tales are fact or myth, the stones excavated by German amateur archaeologist Heinrich Schliemann are real enough: nine layers of different cities on the same site, from a Bronze Age settlement of about 3000 BC to the Greco-Roman metropolis that

GOLD DIGGER

Heinrich Schliemann financed his Trojan excavations with a fortune acquired in the California gold rush of 1849. His boyhood dream of locating Homer's Troy was fired by the idea that there was more gold among them there stones in Turkey. What Schliemann called "Priam's Treasure" was smuggled out to Berlin and carried off in turn by the Russians in 1945, reappearing in Moscow's Pushkin Museum in 1993. In the ongoing wrangle about rightful ownership among Turkey, Germany and Russia is the scholars' question as to whether the treasure is not in fact Schliemann's accumulation of booty from all over Asia Minor.

35

disappeared around AD 400. Excavations are still on-going. The scholars' date of 1250 BC would favour Troy VI as most likely scene for the Homeric events, though evidence shows this city was destroyed by earthquake. Others consider Troy VIIa, built on its ruins, to be the best candidate, as it was apparently razed after a war. In either case, apart from ramparts, a tower or two, a paved ramp and a fanciful model of the wooden horse, the remains demand some imagination to reconstitute the royal city coveted by the Greeks. But if you come as Alexander the Great did, with a copy of Homer in your hand, you will surely hear the echo of battle cries from Agamemnon's fleet across the Trojan plain.

Assos

Still more commonly known by its Greek name than the Turkish *Behramkale*, Assos is a tiny port whose hotels and seafood restaurants make it a convenient base for visiting Troy. The harbour's bollards are recycled columns filched from the Temple of Athena (6th century BC) on a hill behind town. Up at the ancient site, you can see other remains of the settlement founded by Greek colonists from the nearby island of Lesbos, only 10 km (6 miles) away.

Ayvalık

Protected by UNESCO as part of Turkey's cultural heritage, handsome mansions from the Ottoman era add to the lively charm of this fishing port, a fast-growing resort for discerning travellers. Besides the beaches south of town, they are attracted to the bustling bazaar, stronghold for traditional Anatolian craftwork, and the street market's country bread, excellent yoghurts, cheeses and high-quality olive oil. There is also regular ferry service in the summer for day trips to Lesbos.

Pergamum

Modern excavations have done much to reveal what, at its zenith, was one the grandest cities in the eastern Mediterranean. The two principal sites—the ancient city-centre of the Acropolis and the Asclepion health spa—stand north and south of the modern town of Bergama.

Acropolis

The Attalid dynasty of philosopher kings built their royal capital in the 4th century BC in a glorious setting of hillside terraces. Only the outline of the great Altar of Zeus remains since the German excavators carried off its monumental friezes to use as the centrepiece of their archaeological museum in Berlin. But the magnificent Theatre, seating 10,000 spectators on its 80 steeply raked rows, is ample consolation. Nearby are remains of the Temple of Athena and the Pergamene Library, which amassed in its heyday a collection of 200,000 books. The massive Roman Corinthian temple of Emperor Trajan is further up the hill.

Asclepion

Pergamum built its health spa to honour Asclepius, Greek god of healing. The processional colonnade led patients to the waters and baths in the hot springs, and to the temples for sleeping cures, complete with dream-interpretation by the priests. Like any modern spa, the Asclepion provided entertainment and relaxation at its own theatre and library. The town's great physician Galen (130–200) worked here, getting plenty of practice as official doctor to the gladiators.

Izmir

The uncompromisingly modern look of Turkey's second port city, known as Smyrna after its reconstruction by Alexander the Great, is a result of the fire of 1922 during the Greco-Turkish War. In two days, it destroyed three-quarters of the buildings. Gone are the Greek, Armenian, Italian, French and Jewish merchants who ran the town under the Ottomans, making way for a bustling new city of industry, commerce—and the naval base for NATO's southeast Mediterranean command.

At the southern end of the palmtree-lined Kordon promenade, now officially known as Atatürk Caddesi, is Izmir's landmark, the Saat Kulesi clocktower, built at the beginning of the 20th century. Konak Bazaar is located among the narrow streets east of the Kordon, and just beyond that are the excavations of the Roman Agora.

5

FIVE SPLENDID ANCIENT MONUMENTS

Among Turkey's many archaeological sites, the most celebrated, like Troy, do not necessarily have the best monuments. Our choice: at **Pergamum**, the spectacularly located Theatre; two at **Ephesus**, the beautifully restored Library of Celsus and the Theatre; at **Didyma**, the gigantic Temple of Apollo; and at the inland site of **Aphrodisias**, the great Stadium.

Hadrian's Temple, one of the splendours of Ephesus.

Archaeological Museum
South of the clocktower, the museum displays a fine collection of Greek and Roman statuary, mosaics, ceramics, metalwork and jewellery in silver and gold.

Ethnographical Museum
In an old stone building next door to the archaeological museum, it reconstitutes the decors and costumes of Smyrna's cosmopolitan heyday and the folklore and craftwork of the Anatolian hinterland.

Kadifekale
Up on the hill southeast of the city centre, this Byzantine and Ottoman citadel encloses a pleasant pine-shaded park and family playground. It offers an outstanding panorama over the whole Bay of Izmir and is the best vantage point from which to view the columns of the Roman Agora. It's especially appealing around sunset.

Çeşme
Perched at the end of the peninsula west of Izmir, this resort is becoming increasingly popular with Turkish families and is also much appreciated by serious windsurfers. The old castle serves as an open-air theatre, and the marina offers day-trip cruises along the coast.

Kuşadası

With its fine golden sands, good seafood and big marina, this boisterous beach resort concentrates strictly—and very well—on the pleasures of the flesh. For those moved by the higher claims of the spirit, the great archaeological sites of Ephesus, Priene, Miletus and Didyma are within easy reach. The best beaches are Tusan and Pamucak north of town, and the closer Kadınlar Denizli to the south, for lovers of the mob scene.

In Kale, the older part of town, just south of Sağlık Caddesi, attractive Ottoman houses have been transformed into bars and restaurants.

Ephesus

Ephesus (Efes) is magnificently preserved; no other site can give a better sense of what an ancient Greco-Roman town actually looked like. As a prosperous port and centre of the great Artemis cult, it became capital of the Roman province of Asia. It has since silted up; now, beginning at the car park, a vast green plain covers the old harbour. The long Arcadian Way leads from there to the Great Theatre seating 20,000, reconstructed for modern music and arts festivals. South of the theatre, Marble (or Sacred) Way with a central gutter passes between the Lower Agora market square and the brothel, with a mosaic decoration suggesting it was a quite handsome establishment. Behind it are the municipal toilets.

On the far side of the junction of Marble Way and Curetes Way is the superb two-storey façade of the Library of Celsus, a memorial to the Roman proconsul Celsus built by his son around AD 135. Nearby are terraced houses from late imperial and early Byzantine times. Curetes (Priests) Way curves around between the temples of Hadrian and Domitian on its way to the Prytaneum town hall and the Upper Agora market square.

Set in the mountains east of the main site, the Cave of the Seven Sleepers evokes an early Christian legend of seven young men who were shut up there by a pagan emperor and awakened 200 years later to discover that Christianity had become the state religion.

Selçuk

The town closest to Ephesus has a first-class Archaeological Museum, noteworthy for its arresting multiple-bosomed Artemis sculptures. On the western outskirts of town, a solitary pillar and a few blocks of granite are all that remain of the Sanctuary of Artemis, one of the seven wonders of the ancient world to 39

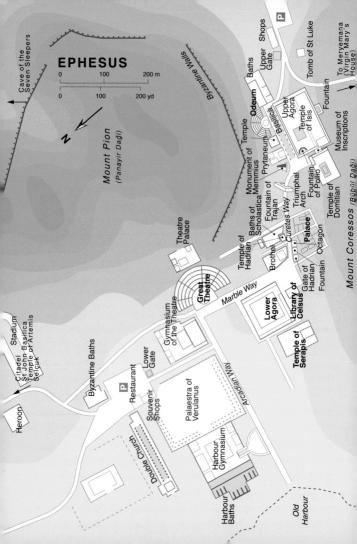

EPHESUS

0   100   200 m
0   100   200 yd

N

Cave of the Seven Sleepers

Mount Pion
(*Panayir Dağı*)

Byzantine Walls

Upper Shops
P
Upper Gate
Baths
Tomb of St Luke
To Meryemana (Virgin Mary's House)

Monument of Memmius
Temple
Odeum
Basilica
Upper Agora
Temple of Isis
Fountain
Museum of Inscriptions

Prytaneum
Baths of Scholastica
Fountain of Trajan
Triumphal Arch
Fountain of Pollio
Temple of Domitian
Curetes Way
Palace
Octagon

Theatre Palace

Temple of Hadrian
Brothel
Gate of Hadrian
Fountain

Mount Coressos (Bülbül Dağı)

Marble Way
Gymnasium of the Theatre
Great Theatre
Lower Agora
Library of Celsus
Temple of Serapis

Citadel
St John Basilica
Temple of Artemis
Selçuk
Stadium

Heroon

Byzantine Baths

Restaurant
P
Lower Gate
Souvenir Shops
Double Church

Arcadian Way

Palaestra of Verulanus

Harbour Gymnasium

Harbour Baths

Old Harbour

which worshippers flocked from all over the Mediterranean. Another pilgrimage shrine, in a pretty mountain setting just outside Selçuk, is the so-called Virgin Mary's House *(Meryemana)*. A small chapel is built on the foundations of a 1st-century dwelling presumed to be Mary's last resting place, such as it appeared to a devout German nun in a vision 1,800 years later. The pilgrims who come here believe Mary accompanied the evangelist St John to this area. His burial place is marked by remains of the 6th-century Basilica of St John.

Three Ionian Cities

The three ancient Greek sites of Priene, Miletus and Didyma can be managed together on one day trip from Kuşadası.

Priene

Like the port of Ephesus, the harbour of Priene silted up. The town has been excavated on an exquisite pine-wooded hillside. Among its more impressive edifices are a square-built council hall, the bouleterion, an Ionic-columned Temple of Athena, and a theatre with five marble thrones for VIPs.

Miletus

Once one of the most powerful cities of the ancient world, needing four harbours for its enormous merchant fleet, Miletus today has only a few Roman structures: a fine theatre seating 15,000, the monumental Nymphaeum fountain on the Sacred Way and the Baths of Faustina. (The huge gateway to the Agora marketplace has, like Pergamum's Altar of Zeus, found its way to Berlin.)

Didyma

In ancient times, the Temple of Apollo existed as one vast sanctuary inhabited only by the priests, with no town around it. War, earthquake, prohibitive building costs and finally the advent of Christianity prevented the edifice ever being completed. But even in its present ruined state up on its elevated platform, the shrine remains a formidable sight. Stand among the pillars and stumps of what were 108 Ionic columns to understand the ancients' concept of their shrine as a stylized forest.

Pamukkale

Make an overnight stay of the excursion inland to this natural white alabaster-like wonderland whose Turkish name translates as "Cotton Castle". On a plateau 100 m (328 ft) over the valley, above the town of Denizli, the gleaming basins and stalactites have been created over the centuries by hot mineral cascades

41

The terraced pools and petrified waterfalls of Pamukkale.

transforming calcium carbonate into travertine. At sunset the white turns magically to gold, pink or carmine. Remove your shoes and wade into the basins or, at one of the hotels on the plateau, take a soothing swim in the mineral pools. The water has been easing away travellers' aches and pains since the dawn of time.

Beside remains of the Temple of Apollo, the nearby archaeological site of Hierapolis includes an imposing Roman Theatre, which hosts the Pamukkale festival in June. It provides a splendid view over the surrounding countryside.

Aphrodisias

This ancient sanctuary to the goddess of love is still being excavated on its plateau beautifully located 600 m (2,000 ft) above the sea; it is well worth the stop on your way to or from Pamukkale. Orthodox Christians transformed the Temple of Aphrodite into a Byzantine church, but it has now been restored to its former pagan state, though only 14 of the original 40 columns remain. Most striking of the monuments is the handsomely preserved Stadium in which 30,000 spectators watched music and drama performances as well as sporting events.

Bodrum

Among Aegean resorts, Bodrum is Turkey's upmarket version of the typical Greek town of dazzling white houses around a picturesque harbour. Here, too, are luxury yachts, an elegant, cosmopolitan clientele, and the usual bouncing night life. As ancient Halicarnassus, it was the birthplace of Greek historian Herodotus. King Mausolus had his burial shrine built here in 355 BC and bequeathed to the world the generic name of *mausoleum*. It is now just a rubble-strewn open-air museum, nearly everything destroyed by earthquake or carried off either as masonry and ornament for the nearby castle or as archaeological booty for the British Museum in London.

The Castle

Up on its promontory high above the harbour, the fortress was built by the Knights of St John in the 15th century as a counterpart to their strongholds on the nearby islands of Kos and Rhodes. The towers were allotted to four nationalities—English, German, Italian and French, the latter serving as a dungeon with a torture chamber denoted by the inscription *Inde Deus Abest* ("Here, God is Absent"). But the pride of the castle is its wonderful museum of underwater archaeology and of treasures salvaged from the region's shipwrecks and other sites. The hull of a two-masted ship which sank in 1025 has been painstakingly reconstructed and put on display, along with jewellery, glassware and amphoras recovered from a wreck found in Serçe harbour south of Bodrum. Another hall is devoted to treasure found at a Bodrum construction site with the sarcophagus and skeleton of a Carian princess of the 4th century BC. Identified by scholars as Ada, stepmother to Alexander the Great, she was accompanied in death by three gold rings, two necklaces, two bracelets, a crown—and a mouse which got trapped in the sarcophagus.

Marmaris

Set where the blue Aegean mingles with the turquoise waters of the Mediterranean, Marmaris basks in the sun below pine-covered hills. The town is prouder of its beaches and marina than the 16th-century fortress, though the latter has developed as a setting for the summer arts festival (music, folk dancing and exhibitions). Besides water sports by day and discos by night, Marmaris is a popular starting-point for boat cruises around the sharply indented peninsula. This is also the best way to get out to more secluded beaches such as Turunç and Kumlubük.

43

Ankara, Hattuşaş (Boğazkale), Yazılıkaya,
Alacahöyük, Amasya, Tokat, Sivas, Kangal,
Gordion, Pessinus, Safranbolu

The terrain between Cappadocia and the Black Sea must have seemed like home from home to the Selçuk Turks, but also to their ancient predecessors, the Hittites, both originally nomadic herders and warriors from the steppes of Central Asia. The seemingly endless rolling plains offered open battlefields for waves of marauding invaders: after the Hittites came Midas's Phrygians, the Persians, Alexander's Greeks, Augustus's Romans, and the armies of the Byzantine Empire; after the Selçuk Turks came the Crusaders, Tamerlane's Mongols and then the Ottoman Turks.

Besides Ankara itself, the capital's hinterland presents fascinating vestiges of the heartland's past: the Hittite strongholds at Boğazkale and Alacahöyük, the Phrygian towns of Gordion and Pessinus, the Selçuk and Ottoman towns of Amasya, Tokat and Sivas, and the breeding place of the great Anatolian sheepdogs known here after their "hometown", Kangal.

Ankara

The city has two sectors: its historic nucleus branching out from the ancient citadel and the modern governmental capital that sprang up around it in the 20th century. Its population now numbers close to 3 million. In its older quarter, the national capital hosts museums devoted to the ancient civilizations of Anatolia and the folklore of the Ottoman Empire. At the heart of the modern town—Yenişehir—south of the citadel, the lively university population offsets the politicians and diplomats in the bars and cafés of the Kızılay district.

The Citadel

Much of the town's history is here. With a splendid view of the city and surrounding countryside, the battlemented Byzantine and Ottoman Ak Kale (White Castle) stands on a hilltop site first commandeered by the Hittites. It is defended by inner and outer ramparts which make use of massive basalt blocks taken from the town's ancient Roman monuments. On the outer walls' southern gate, Hisar Kapısı, is an inscription from the Mongol invasion. Inside, a whole neighbourhood of 19th-century Ottoman houses now occupies the castle precincts along narrow cobbled lanes winding up the side of the hill. Some of the fancier mansions have been converted into restaurants.

Aslanhane Camii

A short walk southeast of the Citadel, this most venerable of Ankara's mosques is a truly fine example of Selçuk architecture. The brick minaret was built in 1290. The mosque takes its name, meaning Lion House, from the ancient Roman carved lions embedded in the octagonal mausoleum *(türbe)* of its founder, Ahi Şerafettin, opposite. The imposing prayer hall has a "forest" of 24 wooden columns, most of them with Corinthian stone capitals taken from ancient Roman temples and Byzantine churches. Note the handsome blue enameltiled prayer niche *(mihrab)* and carved walnut pulpit *(mimber)*.

Museum of Anatolian Civilisations

Southwest of the Citadel, two 15th-century Ottoman buildings have been thoroughly restored and spruced up for the modern needs of one of Turkey's most important museums *(Anadolu Medeniyetleri Müzesi)*. One, the Mahmut Paşa Bedesten, original-

Basalt relief of the god Haldi, Kingdom of Urartu, Eastern Anatolia, 8th century BC.

ly a storehouse for Angora wool, provides the exhibition space, the other, Kurshunlu Han, a merchants' hostelry, houses a library, workshop and offices. The museum assembles collections from all over Turkey, but is best known for the world's most comprehensive collection of Hittite culture.

It is worth following the ground-floor collections, labelled in English, counter-clockwise as they trace Anatolian history from the Stone Age (Palaeolithic, to 10,000 BC, and Neolithic, after 6000 BC) through the Hatti, Assyrians and Hittites to the Phrygians, Urartians and Lydians. In

WHY ON EARTH ANKARA?

When the new republic of Turkey was founded in 1923, Istanbul's sophisticates and especially the foreign diplomats were not at all happy to see Atatürk making Ankara the new capital. For those prepared to read them, the country's bold new leader had already given the signals. It was from this historic battleground of the Turks' turbulent rise to nationhood that Atatürk chose in 1919 to lead his resistance against both the Ottoman sultan and the invading Greek army. However much more appropriate cosmopolitan Istanbul might have seemed for his aspirations to modernity, Atatürk understood the need to engage this Asia Minor heartland in the enterprise of cutting free from its feudal past and linking Turkey's destiny to Europe.

In fact, Ankara had not always been the sleepy provincial backwater to which the Ottomans had reduced it by the beginning of the 20th century. The town was founded by the Hittites as Ankuwash in the 12th century BC, thriving from its key location on the trade route between their capital, Hattuşaş, and the Persian city of Sardis. Occupied briefly by Gallic tribes in the 2nd century BC, it remained a prosperous market town throughout Roman antiquity, numbering over 200,000 inhabitants by the 3rd century AD. Under the Byzantines, it sank almost into oblivion except for the continuing trade in the prized wool of its Angora goats. In 1402 it was the scene of a momentous battle in which the Mongols' mighty Tamerlane defeated the Ottoman sultan Bayezid I. Many believe that the humiliating memory of the sultan's imprisonment—"Mongol" became a taboo word throughout the Ottoman era—also played a part in Atatürk's choice of Ankara as capital in the process of restoring national self-confidence.

the basement galleries are Greek and Roman antiquites and Ankara's own ancient artefacts. Here are the highlights.

Stone Age: terracotta statue, 5750 BC, of a Mother Goddess giving birth on her throne, tended by two leopards, from the Çatalhüyük site 50 km (30 miles) southeast of Konya; deer- and pig-shaped oil vessels, 5500 BC, from Hacılar, north of Antalya.

Hatti: bronze stag and bull statuettes, ceremonial sun-disks, and golden cups, jugs and jewellery, all Bronze Age, 3rd millennium BC, Alacahöyük near Boğazkale.

Assyrian: merchants' clay tablets and envelopes inscribed with cuneiform writing, 19th century BC, Kültepe site near Kayseri.

Hittite: elegant beak-spouted jugs, bull's head ritual vessels; clay tablets, stone and bronze plaques with cuneiform and hieroglyphic writing; gold jewellery; monumental stone reliefs of warriors, religious processions and gate lions, 1700–700 BC, from Boğasköy, Alacahöyük and Kargamiş (now part of Syria).

Phrygian: in recreated timber-framed royal burial chamber, wooden table, children's toys, painted ceramics, bronze vessels, from Gordion, 8th century BC.

Temple of Augustus

West of the Citadel just north of Hisarparkı Caddesi, the town's most important Roman monument was built in the reign of Emperor Augustus around 20 BC and is famous for bearing, almost completely intact, an inscription of his political testament. It stands on the site of an earlier temple dedicated to the Phrygian goddess Cybele and moon god Men. With a portico originally numbering eight Corinthian columns east and west and fifteen on the sides, it served subsequently as a Christian church in the 5th century and an Islamic seminary *(medrese)* in the 15th century for the adjacent Hacı Bayram Mosque. The imperial inscription of the emperor's deeds, RERUM GESTARUM DIVI AUGUSTI, is written in Latin on the wall to the left of the vestibule and in Greek on the right. The eastern wall was pierced with three windows for the crypt of the Christian church.

Julian's Column

West of the Temple of Augustus on Hükümet Meydanı, the column celebrates a visit by Emperor Julian in AD 362. Christians dubbed him the Apostate because of his abortive efforts to revive worship of the Roman gods. Muslims nicknamed the column the Belkıs Minaresi (Queen of Sheba's Minaret), and storks have now made it their home, building a nest on its Corinthian capital.

Roman Baths

The sprawling complex of ancient public baths and gymnasium (1st century AD) is incongruously surrounded by modern apartment blocks on Çankırı Caddesi, northwest of Julian's Column. Signposts identify the *caldarium* (hot rooms), *tepidarium* (warm rooms), *frigidarium* (cold rooms) and swimming pool. Apart from the water-heating furnaces and a few walls and arches of dressing rooms, the only recognizable structures are the low stone and brick columns forming the floor-heating system.

War of Independence Museum

Of the many museums and monuments devoted to the creation of the Turkish republic and its modern achievements, this (*Kürtülüş Savaş Müzesi*) is the most interesting to foreign visitors. On Ulus Meydanı west of the Citadel, it is housed in the republic's first National Assembly. The classroom appearance of the parliamentary chamber has been preserved, with the rows of delegates' school desks surrounding the platform on which Atatürk presided. Documents, photographs and weapons trace the heroic events of the republic's foundation.

Ethnographic Museum

On Talat Paşa Caddesi, the handsome white marble museum presents most of its collections of Anatolian folk culture—ornaments, costumes, furniture and utensils—in the recreated settings of Ottoman households. Artistically, the most impressive exhibits are the carved Islamic *mimber* (pulpits), *mihrab* (prayer niches) and *türbe* (tombs) from the region's mosques.

Atatürk Mausoleum

The Father of the Turks is buried in a heavily symbolic national shrine on a landscaped hill southwest of the city centre. The monumental approach is flanked by Independence Tower to the right, with statues of three men, and Liberty Tower to the left, with statues of three women, all epitomizing the Turkish people. Beyond them, an avenue of 24 neo-Hittite granite lions leads to an esplanade with four other allegorical towers, a gallery enclosing the tomb of the republic's second president, Ismet Inönü, and a museum of Atatürk's personal possessions and photographs. Atatürk's mausoleum (*Anıtkabir*) is a massive porticoed temple of square-cut travertine pillars surrounding a marble hall with his tomb at the centre.

Kızılay and the Modern City

South of the citadel, Ankara's liveliest entertainment area, at least for university students and the younger crowd in general, is centred on and around the bars, cafés and restaurants of Kızılay district's Sakarya Caddesi and Bayındır Sokak.

Further south, fashionable boutiques, major hotels and the smarter restaurants extend along Atatürk Bulvarı, which becomes Embassy Row with the glitzy Karum shopping mall at its southern end. Just before the Presidential Palace, Çankaya Caddesi curves southwest to Atakule, a reinforced concrete and glass tower with a smart shopping centre at the bottom and grand view from the observation platform at the top at 125 m (410 ft), reachable by express lift.

Hattuşaş

Just north of the town of Boğazkale, some 200 km (125 miles) east of Ankara, the huge site of the Hittites' ancient capital sprawls across a sloping mountain plateau rising between two valleys. Excavations began only in 1906. The rugged terrain is dotted with several outcrops of limestone which the Hittites skilfully incorporated into the building of the city's fortresses. A loop road makes it possible to drive around the site from one monument to another—temples, fortresses, city-gates—but you should also be prepared to do some walking, in good shoes.

The village of Boğazkale, also known by its old name of Boğazköy, has a small museum of Hattuşaş ceramics and cuneiform tablets, but the excavations' major findings, including the originals of many statues seen here as replicas, are displayed at the Ankara Museum of Anatolian Civilisations.

Great Temple

From the ticket office, a modern road between scant remains of the city's northwest gate and ancient storehouses leads to the main temple, Büyük Mabet. Here, as in the city's other monuments, the structures' inner walls of timber and sun-dried mud brick have gone, and only stone foundations 49 and some outer walls survive. Two limestone blocks mark the ceremonial gateway from which stone paving traces the ancient processional route followed by the Hittite king and queen in their roles of high priest and priestess. Notice the rectangular stone basins used for ritual ablution, one of them with the remains of a sculpted lion. The paved route leads to a central courtyard surrounded by twelve chambers. Two were shrines for the Hittites' principal deities, Teshub the weather or storm god and Hepatu the sun goddess. Others were prayer-cells for priests and storerooms for oil and grain kept in large earthenware jars, *pithoi*.

Fortress

Beyond the Great Temple, the road forks right uphill, passing to the east the formidable ruin of Yenicekale, a fortress built from massive limestone blocks hewn from the cliff, 30 m (98 ft) high, on which it stands.

City Gates and Walls

Aslankapı (Lion Gate), west of Yenicekale, stands at the beginning of the imposing fortifications defending the city's southern border. The gate is flanked by two stone lions (originals in the Ankara Museum). The dry-stone city walls were built on a sloping embankment paved with rough-hewn limestone slabs, and measuring in some places 15 m (49 ft) in height and 75 m (246 ft) wide at the base.

Yerıkapı (Earth Gate), to the east, is also known as the Sphinx Gate because of two mighty sphinxes that once guarded it—now on show in museums in Istanbul and Berlin—and two smaller ones, still here but somewhat weathered. Beneath the gate, a stone corbelled tunnel runs from the city through the embankment to the countryside beyond.

Kralkapı (King's Gate), in the southeast corner, has a figure carved on the left pillar with pointed helmet and raised left fist (original in Ankara). This is in fact not a king but the weather god Teshub.

Nişantepe and Sarikale

From Kralkapı, the road descends north to a rock face inscribed with hieroglyphics (Nişantepe means Inscription Hill) dating back to 1200 BC. The 10-line inscription is believed to be a declaration of or about the last known Hittite king, Suppiliuma II, who name appears at the beginning. To the west, on top of a precipice 50 m (164 ft) high, Sarikale (Yellow Fortress) has sturdy inner walls of ashlar stone from the 14th century BC, but the outer walls and gate were probably Phrygian additions.

Great Fortress

East of the loop road, Büyük Kale is the royal citadel of Hattuşaş, built in the 14th century BC and forming part of the city's northern fortifications. On its northeast side, a sheer cliff drops away to the Büyükkaya Gorge. A modern stairway has replaced the ancient ramp, taking you up to the vast plateau, 250 m (820 ft) long and 140 m (459 ft) wide, on which the citadel was built on three levels. Around the lower courtyard were the royal offices and guardrooms, while the royal apartments were arranged around the middle and upper courtyards. The royal archives were also here; when discovered they were found to contain 2,500 cuneiform texts, including the famous Hittite-Egyptian Peace Treaty.

Yazılıkaya

Just 3 km (2 miles) east of Hattuşaş, two narrow ravines have been transformed into carved rock galleries to serve as sanctuaries for the royal capital's celebrations of the New Year, which began in the spring.

Great Gallery

The carved reliefs on the larger gallery's left wall shows a procession of male divinities wearing belted kilts and carrying a mace or scimitar. They are led by the weather god Teshub. Carrying a mace and sword, he stands on the bowed necks of two mountain gods on the far wall of the gallery. Teshub greets the sun goddess Hepatu, standing on a panther, with their son Sharruma, also on a panther. They lead a

---

RISE AND FALL

The town's name of Hattuşaş recalls its original founders, the Hatti, who settled here around 2500 BC, along with a colony of Assyrian merchants. The town was destroyed by the Hittite king Anitta in 1720 BC and reconstructed a century later. The Hittite kings later liked the name well enough to adopt it as their own. It was King Hattuşaşili III who negotiated a famous peace treaty with Egypt's pharaoh Ramses II in 1259 BC, of which the cuneiform text was found here in the royal citadel. It divides control of the eastern Mediterranean between Egyptians and Hittites after the latter had stopped Ramses at Kadesh on his advance into Asia Minor. The Hittites' proud capital—and with it their empire—was destroyed after the invasion in 1200 BC of Mediterranean raiders whom historians can identify only as the Sea People. The Phrygians rebuilt the city around 650 BC, but it never retrieved its ancient splendour.

procession of goddesses carved on the gallery's right wall; their hair is braided and they wear long robes and belted cloaks. Near the entrance behind the goddesses is a tall relief of King Tudhaliya IV (1250–1220 BC) with round cap, coat and cape, probably the patron of these rock carvings.

Small Gallery

Over to the right, stairs lead up to this smaller ravine with reliefs in a much better state of preservation. The gallery is believed to be the mortuary temple of King Tudhaliya. It is guarded by two winged demons with lion's head and human body. On the west wall are 12 scimitar-wielding gods of the underworld marching in single file. At the south end of the other wall, the king is shown being embraced by the god Sharruma. On the same wall is a symbolic figure of a huge sword blade known as the Sword God.

Alacahöyük

Some 25 km (16 miles) north of Boğazkale, the site of this ancient Hatti city has produced a magnificent collection of gold jewellery and bronze statues of bulls, stags, the earth goddess and the sundisks that became a monumental emblem for modern Turkey. A good selection of these are displayed in the local museum next to the archaeological site (with many more exhibited at the Ankara Museum). Most of the city's remains date from its Hittite period—notably the Sphinx Gate, with its two stone sphinxes and a two-headed eagle carved on the right gate-post. The reliefs carved on either side of the gate depict a religious procession of a king and queen bringing sacrifices to the god Teshub. Inside the gate, signposts lead to remains of Hittite temples and a palace and a necropolis of 13 Hatti tombs.

Amasya

This most charming of northern Anatolian towns some 80 km (50 miles) from the Black Sea is located in a deep gorge of the Yeşil river valley. The river running through the city is bordered by handsome Ottoman mansions and mosques, overlooked by an august castle ruin and rock-cut tombs on the mountainside rising above the north bank.

One of Turkey's most ancient towns, it traces its settlement back to 5500 BC. It had been the capital of the Pontic kingdom established at the end of the 4th century BC in the wake of Alexander's conquests. Amasya was the birthplace of the renowned Greek geographer and historian Strabo (64 BC–c.23 AD), and subsequently home to many Turkish scholars, scientists and poets. It also provided a training school for such future Ottoman sultans as Murat II, Bayezid II and Selim, crown princes who served here as governors.

Mosque Complex

Set amid rose gardens and orchards leading down to the Yeşil river, Sultan Bayezid II Külliye centres on a 15th-century mosque (1485) comprising two large domes flanked by two minarets and nine cupolas forming the roof of an elegant arcade. The complex includes a *medrese* (seminary), a library, a soup kitchen for the poor and a mausoleum.

Archaeological and Ethnographic Museum

Housed in a modern building on Mustafa Kamal Paşa Caddesi, *Amasya Müzesi* combines its collection of Hittite, Greek and Roman antiquities with fine examples of local Islamic art. One of the highlights is a Selçuk elaborately carved door from the Gök Medrese (Blue Seminary). There is also a collection of Ottoman furniture, costumes and weapons.

Birmarhane Hospital

This rare example of Mongol architecture was built after the invasion of 1308 as a treatment centre for mental health. Belying the received image of Mongol "barbarians", it has a magnificently carved entrance and graceful open-air arcaded courtyard. Its carved depictions of the human figure have been defaced by Islamic zealots. The hospital now serves as a music academy, all the more appropriate since the soothing sounds of music—and the running water of fountains—were an integral part of the original therapy.

Riverside Houses

The north bank of the Yeşil is lined with 19th-century patrician mansions *(konak)*, some of them half-timbered, with the upper storeys leaning out over the river for the most advantageous view. Outstanding is the Hazeranlar Konak, built by the provincial treasurer in 1865, now open to the public as a museum of fine art and local folklore.

In the side streets behind it are many more modest but charming examples of old Ottoman housing.

Büyük Ağa Medrese

Also on the river's north bank, on the east side of town, this impressive 15th-century domed octagonal structure still operates as a theological seminary, but the public is allowed in discreetly to view the fine arcaded courtyard.

Rock Tombs

On the mountainside behind the houses are monumental tombs hewn in the limestone rockface. According to Strabo, they were the last resting place of many kings of Pontus. Some were later used by the Byzantines as Christian sanctuaries.

Castle

Built on eight levels, the castle ruin sprawling across its mountain is worth the climb for the grand view from the top. The citadel (*kale*) was first built in classical antiquity and restored many times by Amasya's Byzantine and Ottoman rulers. A disused "secret" stone tunnel (*cilanbolu*) runs from the highest castle keep down to the city.

Tokat

Southeast of Amasya along the Yeşil river, the town nestles at the foot of a hilltop Pontic castle ruin. The city centre's most distinctive building is the multiple-domed bathhouse, Ali Paşa Hamamı, on a busy square opposite the black domed Ali Paşa mosque. The charm of Tokat's older quarters can best be enjoyed among the traditional Ottoman houses along the quiet lanes extending east of the bathhouse. Two outstanding houses are Madimağin Celalin Konak in the Muftu quarter and Latifoğlu Konak, now a museum.

A good museum of Anatolian folklore is housed in the Gök Medrese (Blue Seminary). In what were once the students' dormitories and classrooms, it exhibits looms and fabrics of the town's traditional textile manufacture, along with furniture, carpets and costumes, as well as Hittite, Greek and Roman artefacts, ceramics and sculpture.

The town's best-loved monument, famous throughout Anatolia, is its local delicacy, much copied but never equalled, the Tokat kebab of oven-baked lamb chops, bell peppers, aubergine, tomatoes and potatoes.

Sivas

This big modern bustling town (population approaching 250,000) has a historic centre of impressive 13th-century edifices dating back to its heyday under the Selçuks' Sultanate of Rum.

Just south of the main city square, the Bürüciye Medresesi was completed in 1271 and now houses a market for carpet salesmen and booksellers along with a café out in the courtyard. The neighbouring Çifte Minare Medrese (Twin Minaret Seminary), built in the same year, has a spectacular carved façade from which rise its two brick minarets with just a few of the original blue tiles. Opposite, the place to stop for refreshments is the Şifaiye Medresesi, a medical college and hospital founded by the Selçuk sultan Kaykâvus in 1217, and now a colourful bazaar with capets and kilims decorating a charming tea garden. The sultan's family tomb, with tiled sarcophagi, is to the right of the entrance.

The finest of the city's Selçuk buildings is the Gök Medrese (also 1271), south on Cumhuriyet Caddesi. Sadly, its graceful minarets show only traces of their blue-tiled ornament, but the carving and ceramic-tile ornament on the façade is particularly splendid.

Kangal

Some 70 km (44 miles) south of Sivas are the kennels of the great Kangal sheepdogs, a breed that traces its origins back to the 3rd century BC. The journey to their breeding grounds is for some dog-lovers as reverential as any pilgrimage to Rome or Jerusalem.

These magnificent golden-haired beasts are monuments of intelligence, strength and fidelity.

Gordion

The site near the village of Yassihöyük, 96 km (60 miles) west of Ankara, was the capital of the Phrygian kingdom during its heyday in the 8th century BC. Its strategic position on the ancient route between Troy and Antioch in Syria made it a gateway to Asia. On the acropolis west of the village, the monumental Phrygian Gate of limestone blocks, originally coated with a layer of smooth white stucco, leads to government offices, workshops, storehouses, and a palace with four great halls. The buildings excavated by German and American archaeologists are identified by an orientation plan overlooking the site. The northernmost palace-hall *(megaron)* is believed to have served as a temple to the goddess Cybele, in which the Gordian knot was notoriously cut by Alexander the Great on his path of conquest.

Royal Tomb

East of the acropolis is the Phrygian necropolis of mound tombs. The largest, in a mound 53 m (179 ft) high and 300 m (984 ft) in diameter, is known as the Royal Tomb. The skeleton found inside, a man in his early sixties, 55 has long been thought to be that of King Midas, but archaeologists now argue that it might have been a predecessor. He was buried around 700 BC with bronze cauldrons, utensils, tables and other furniture. The burial chamber has a gabled roof of finely hewn pine beams and walls of massive juniper logs, making it perhaps the oldest standing wooden structure in the world. Opposite the Royal Tomb, the village museum exhibits some sculpture and ceramics from the site, but most of Gordion's treasures are now displayed in Ankara's Museum of Anatolian Civilisations.

Pessinus

Just outside the modern village of Ballıhisar 60 km (37 miles) southwest of Gordion are the remains of the sanctuary dedicated

THE ALEXANDER TOUCH

Gordius was just a poor Phrygian peasant crossing Anatolia in an ox-cart when he founded the town now bearing his name. An eagle perched on the cart persuaded local priests that this fellow had the right stuff to be their king. Gordius tied up his cart in the temple and an oracle proclaimed that anyone able to undo the yoke's divinely blessed knot, of tough rawhide thongs, would be lord of Asia.

Midas came along, a pleasure-loving man from Macedonia with a taste for music and Dionysian dancing whom childless Gordius chose as his heir. Midas preferred not to mess with the knot, having had his share of trouble with divine "blessings". Dionysius had all too literally granted him a wish that everything he touched would turn to gold—not just his furniture and stones in the garden, but his food, water and daughter, too—until he was released from the cursed wish. Then, at a music contest of the gods, Midas had dared not to prefer Apollo, who promptly gave him a pair of donkey's ears. Forget the knot.

Alexander, another fellow from Macedonia—this much is history— stopped off in Gordion in 333 BC. While awaiting reinforcements in his campaign against the Persians, he heard about the ox-cart tied up in the temple. Ever the showman, he decided to save his momentous tussle with the knot for the eve of his departure. With thousands of troops waiting outside, he tugged and heaved at the sacred knot and got nowhere. Enough of this religious nonsense, he had a world to conquer, drew his sword, cut the knot in two and went off to India.

to the Phrygian earth goddess Cybele. Excavations have uncovered the massive stone blocks of the temple's foundations along with its four-square inner sanctum. Nearby is a theatre at which orgiastic rituals are said to have been performed, where frenzied novices sacrificed their genitals to the goddess. The Romans maintained the site in gratitude for the part the goddess is believed to have played in saving Rome from defeat by Hannibal in the 3rd century BC, after a sacred black meteorite associated with her cult had been transported to the imperial capital—minus the theatrical orgies.

Safranbolu

Though it is 220 km (38 miles) from Ankara, this beautifully preserved old Ottoman town up in the hill country, barely 80 km (50 miles) inland from the Black Sea, is more easily visited from the Turkish capital than from the major Black Sea resorts. And it is well worth the drive. Listed as a UNESCO World Cultural Heritage site in 1994, the town has lovingly maintained its bazaar, public baths and elegant 18th- and 19th-century half-timbered houses. A few display to the public their plush quarters reserved for male guests (*selamlik*), the more cosy lattice-windowed women's apartments (*harem*), the shared family quarters for cooking, dining and sleeping, and the children's playroom. Some have been converted to hotels, enabling you to spend a night in the old style, while others preserve their old-fashioned privacy. Quite as much as foreign visitors, Turkish tourists enjoy this glimpse of the way things used to be.

To get to the charming old district of Safranbolu, known as Çarşi, on the east side of a ravine, the Ankara road passes through the decidedly ugly modern district of Kiranköy. Right on Çarşi Meydanı, the main square, are the public baths, Cinci Hamam, with separate facilities for men and women—a good place to end your afternoon if you are planning to do a lot of walking. The Yemeniciler Arastası bazaar and old houses fan out in every direction along narrow cobbled streets and lanes up and down hill. This is a place to get gloriously lost and found again. One old house to look out for, signposted at strategic points, is Kaymakamlar Evi, the Governor's House, which has now been transformed into a museum.

During the hot months of July and August, many residents of Safranbolu retreat to their old summer houses, also venerable 18th- and 19th-century mansions, in the Bağlar district northwest of Kiranköy.

Cultural Notes

Atatürk

Literally "Father of the Turks", the name was adopted by the nation's revered Mustafa Kemal in 1934 when ordering all citizens to use a surname rather than, say, traditional combinations of son's and father's first names. As part of his Westernization programme, Atatürk (1881–1938) personally conducted lessons in public parks in how to use the Latin rather than Arabic alphabet. He also set an example in modern dress, replacing his old fez with a black European homburg. But in outlawing polygamy as part of female emancipation, he did not curtail his own compulsive womanizing.

Coffee-houses

More or less out of bounds to women, the most lively *kahvehane* are around or right inside the bazaar. Today, tea rather than coffee is served, strong and sugared in tulip glasses. The men play dominoes, introduced to Istanbul by Venetian merchants, or backgammon *(tavla)*, which originated in ancient Babylon and Egypt. Customers puff away at a *nargile* of compressed Persian tobacco, lit by embers of charcoal, with the smoke cooled through a long lamb's-leather tube. For a more "Western" allure, some prefer the yellowish clay-like meerschaum pipe.

Crescent and Star

The emblem of Islam originated when Istanbul was Byzantium. In 340 BC, Philip II of Macedonia's surprise attack on the city was foiled after the moon broke through the clouds and revealed his army's presence. In gratitude, the people adopted Hecate, goddess of the night, and put her symbols of crescent and star on their city's coins.

Grease wrestling

The best known of the *yağlı güreş* tournaments is Edirne's Kırkpınar Festival, usually held in June. During the warm-up exercises, gypsies play the *zurna* (oboe) and beat the *davul* (bass drum). Clad in leather shorts, the wrestlers are doused from head to toe in olive oil. Several elimination bouts go on simultaneously. It may take a few minutes or two hours for the winner to pin his opponent's back to the ground. There are four categories, and the greatest honour is the Golden Belt.

Güney, Yilmaz (1937–85)

This leading figure in Turkish cinema made many movies by smuggling out scripts and directing instructions while he was imprisoned from 1971 to 1974 by the military regime. His most famous film, *Yol* (The Road), is a harsh indictment of modern Turkish society. In *Sürü* (The Herd), he depicted the upheavals of peasants moving to the cities, and in *Duvar* (The Wall), the injustices of imprisonment.

Hamam

The Turkish bath has separate hours for men *(erkekler)* and for women *(kadınlar)*. Bathers are given wooden clogs and a cotton wrap for wandering around the hamam—and a proper towel for drying later. The steam bath is followed by the climactic massage up on a heated stone slab. After the pummelling and pressing, you may be treated to an equally vigorous body scrub with an abrasive glove to get rid of dead skin. Finish off the experience with tea, fruit juice or mineral water to counter dehydration.

Kilim

This subtly patterned flat woven rug, without pile, is the oldest of all Turkish carpets. It is depicted on murals in the Stone Age village of Çatalhüyük (6500 BC). Its motifs and colours have age-old symbols: red means goodness and wealth, blue is for nobility, green for paradise, yellow and black for protection against the evil eye.

Shadow puppets

Made of camel hide or cardboard, the puppet figures date back to the 14th-century Sultan Orhan. Stonemason Karagöz and blacksmith Hacivat, working on a mosque in Bursa, were notorious for their irreverent banter. When fellow workers downed tools to listen, the sultan ordered them both beheaded. Regretting his hasty cruelty, Orhan had them immortalized as shadow puppets. They have been playing out their comedy ever since.

Yalı

The Turkish gentry began building these elegant wooden country villas along the shores of the Golden Horn and the Bosphorus in the 17th and 18th centuries. The diplomatic corps subsequently took them over as ambassadorial residences and consulates. They have a distinctive ornate style of turrets, gables and balconies with plenty of Venetian-blinded windows from which to enjoy the waterfront view. In the 20th century, the Istanbul bourgeoisie adopted the design for their summer houses on the Princes' Islands. 59

Shopping

The Turkish market is the centre of social intercourse. It's the place to meet, have a shoe-shine, haircut or shave, drink a glass of tea. There's less hard sell than you might imagine. Like the offer of tea or coffee, bargaining is as much a social ritual as commercial obligation. That inevitable "Where are you from?" is not just a friendly first question, it's an opening gambit in gauging the sales prospect and appropriate technique—they don't treat a British customer as they would an American.

Where?

The centuries-old covered bazaar is still divided into sections according to trade—jewellery, textiles, leatherware, carpets, and so on. Istanbul's Grand Bazaar is a veritable shopping mall, while the Spice or Egyptian Market sells much more than just traditional spices and exotic foods. Flea markets abound around the Grand Bazaar and over on the Asian shore on Üsküdar's Büyük Hamam street. The city's more fashionable—and expensive—boutiques are located in the Beyoğlu and Şişli districts.

Bursa's covered bazaar is renowned for its silks and textiles.

In Ankara's diplomatic and governmental neighbourhoods, you'll find all the internationally famous fashion boutiques in ultra-modern shopping malls.

What?

To buy things that capture the real atmosphere of Turkey, it's a good idea not to shop before you've gained a feeling for the place. On the practical side, make sure your purchases are not too big or too fragile to pack.

Antiques

It's illegal to export antiquities of artistic or archaeological value, including old carpets, but other antiques such as Ottoman samovars, ornaments, glassware, hookah pipes, even old jewellery are allowed. If there is any doubt, ask an official before you make your purchase. And if you buy a copy that is so perfect that a customs official may *suspect* it to be antique, ask the dealer for an invoice stating the value, where and when the article was made.

Ignore the vendors of old coins or statuary who hang around the ancient sites; whatever they are selling is either fake or illegal.

Carpets and Kilims

Used as floor- or wall-coverings, Turkish carpets are renowned for their brilliant patterns and fine workmanship. The most expensive are of pure silk, but you may prefer fine-tufted wool for everyday use. Unlike knotted carpets, kilims are flat woven without pile. Embroidered kilims are called *cicims*. When you choose the pattern, you may not mind if the motifs symbolize good fortune, piety, love or fertility, but check on the colour dye by discreetly rubbing with a damp white cloth. If it stains the cloth, the colour is artificial.

Ceramics

Kütahya factories have replaced the royal Iznik workshops in producing the brilliantly coloured tiles that used to decorate the sultans' palaces and mosques. They are still a great buy, along with plates, bowls and jugs for which cerulean blue is the most valued colour.

Clothing

The fashion designers of Istanbul have burst onto the international scene with subtle combinations of traditional Turkish and modern Western styles using Bursa silk and angora wool from the Ankara region. In Bursa or Istanbul, you may want to buy a bolt of silk or other fabric to make up back home. The silk headscarves resembling an Iznik tile are stunning. Among peasant clothes, light cotton blouses and headscarves are popular, and the brightly coloured heavy woollen socks are great for winter.

Copper and Brassware

Best buys are hand-crafted samovars, pots and cups for Turkish coffee, candlesticks and lamps. Copper cooking utensils such as tea-kettles should be lined with tin. You'll find the best at Istanbul's copper market outside the Grand Bazaar near the Nuruosmaniye mosque or in bric-a-brac shops at Bergama.

Gourmet Delicacies

Easiest to carry are bottles of *rakı* apéritif or sweetmeats like Turkish delight and *halva* flavoured with pistachio, almond or hazel- 61

Call in at the Spice Market to take home a fragrant reminder of Istanbul.

nut. Don't risk *baklava* or other pastries—the honey will melt and leak in transit, and they're extremely heavy.

Jewellery

The cheapest and most popular jewel is the ceramic or glass blue eye-bead to ward off the Evil Eye. More serious gold and silver jewellery is sold by weight, leaving the quality and design of workmanship, particularly eastern Anatolian filigreed silver, to your personal taste. Amber and turquoise are the most prized of semi-precious stones. For the super-stressed executive, buy worry-beads.

Leatherware

Besides the solid cowhide bags, look for the finest Anatolian lambskin leathers used for coats, jackets and lighter garments. Before buying, check the stitching, sometimes badly finished. Bodrum is renowned for its sandals.

Musical Instruments

The easiest to carry of Turkey's traditional instruments are the *davul* (drum), the *ney* (Dervish flute) and the *saz* (a long-necked lute). For the authentic product, go to Istanbul's workshop outlets on Atatürk Bulvari near the aqueduct, *not* souvenir shops.

Sports

Some people, of course, come to Turkey only for the sports, champing at the bit to go wind-surfing or sailing on the Aegean coast. Others concentrating more on Istanbul might welcome a swim or game of tennis as a relaxing break from sightseeing and shopping.

Water Sports

Kuşadası, Bodrum and Marmaris have superb facilities for sailing, wind-surfing, snorkelling, water-skiing and paragliding. Scuba-diving among the underwater archaeological sites off Bodrum and Marmaris needs official authorization. Besides longer cruises on yachts, chartered with or without a crew, the marinas at these resorts offer day-trip cruises to remoter coves for swimmers seeking a little tranquillity away from the family beaches. One place where the swimming is unforgettable, crowded or not, is in the thermal pools at Pamukkale.

During your Istanbul stay, limit your swimming to the hotel pool, as the water at the nearest beaches on the Bosphorus or Sea of Marmara is likely to be polluted. The Princes' Islands, however, are much safer—Büyükada and especially Heybeliada rank high with serious water sports enthusiasts. Yachts can be chartered at the Ataköy marina on the European shore and Kalaiş marina on the Asian side.

Fishing

You need a licence for spearfishing, but not for line or net fishing off the beach. At Assos and Ayvalık, friendly fishermen may take you out for an early morning's deep-sea fishing. The catch includes sea bass, red mullet, mackerel, spiny lobster, crab and shrimp.

Tennis

Big hotels in Istanbul and at the major Aegean resorts have hard courts, floodlit at night, which is often the most comfortable time to play.

Horseback Riding

At Marmaris and Çeşme, you can hire horses to explore the picturesque trails in the hinterland or ride along the sea shore.

The translucent waters of the jagged southern Aegean coast are perfect for sailing.

Hiking and Skiing

Just 35 km (21 miles) from Bursa, the rivers, lakes and forests of the national park on Uludağ mountain are a great place for rambles from June to September and for winter sports from December to April. The ski resort has slalom and giant slalom courses as well as slopes for beginners. Equipment can be rented on the spot.

Spectator Sports

Football is *the* great national sport, with passions nationwide stoked to fever-pitch by the rivalries of Istanbul's three teams, Galatasaray, Beşiktaş and Fenerbahçe. The fireworks and war cries match anything seen in medieval times between the notorious Blues and Greens at the Byzantine Hippodrome. Watch out, too, for basketball matches, increasingly popular.

For visitors in December or January, camel wrestling tournaments, strangely ballet-like, more folklore than sport, are held at Selçuk, near the ancient site of Ephesus, and at Ayvin, just south of Izmir.

Another national sport is grease wrestling, with contests taking place all through the summer and the main tournament held every June near Edirne.

Dining Out

The Ottoman Empire introduced its cuisine throughout the Mediterranean, so that much of what you find today in Greece, Egypt, Lebanon and further afield in North Africa is of Turkish origin. It is rich and varied—and by no means limited to the all-too-familiar kebabs. Turks are natural hedonists and enjoy their food as much for its colour, texture and aroma as for its sheer nourishment. So besides the usual hotel meals, try to get out to the town restaurants and share the appetizing Turkish experience.

To Start With...

Appetizers, *meze,* can make a whole meal, so just have a taste of each if you want a main course, too. Cold delicacies, eaten with white bread or unleavened *pide*: aubergine mashed with lemon (*patlıcan salatası*) or sliced and sautéed (*patlıcan kızartması*); chopped tomato, cucumber and lettuce (*çoban salatası*); bell peppers, cabbage or vine leaves stuffed with rice, pine nuts and minced meat (*dolma*); dips of salty *tarama* (fish roe paste), tangy *tahina* (ground sesame seed) or cool *cacık* (garlicky yoghurt and chopped cucumber). Warm starters may include fried mussels (*midye tavası*), light pastry stuffed with cheese or meat (*böregi*), or thin-sliced mutton liver (*arnavut ciğeri*).

Fish, Meat or Vegetarian?

Coastal fisheries offer a fine range of fresh seafood: red mullet (*barbunya*), swordfish (*kılıç*), bass (*levrek*), bream (*saragöz*), prawns (*karides*), squid (*kalamar*) and mussels (*midye*). These are best lightly fried or charcoal-grilled. Chips (French fries) will be served if you insist, but the Turks prefer a little salad.

You'll find kebabs galore, of lamb, mutton or beef: familiar *şiş kebap* with tomato, green pepper and onion, spiced-up *Adana kebap*, popular *döner kebap* sliced from its vertical skewer, its rich Bursa variation, *Iskender kebap* drenched in yoghurt gravy, and *Tokat kebap* of lamb chops and vegetables. Turkish gourmets recommend stuffed leg of lamb (*kuzu dolması*) or the hearty *güveç*, a spicy meat and vegetable stew cooked in a clay pot. Try *köfte* (meatballs) or barbecued mutton tripe, *kokoreç*. Roast chickens (*piliç*) are generally small but tasty.

Vegetarians should go for the vegetable stew (*türlü sebze*). Besides the ubiquitous aubergine (*patlıcan*), there are all manner of bean dishes: a solid white bean soup (*kuru fasulye*), green beans in tomato sauce (*zeytinyağlı fasulye*) and broad beans (*bakla*). Look out, too, for okra (*bamya*), spinach (*ispanak*) and cauliflower (*karnıbahar*). But remember: these dishes may be cooked in a meat stock.

Desserts

Turkish sweetmeats are an enduring monument to the wonderful self-indulgence of the Ottoman Empire, a world power that drowned—smiling—in a sea of nuts and fruit dripping with honey and rose syrup. The best known sweets are *baklava*, paper-thin layers of pastry filled with marzipan, honey and pistachios. *Kadayıf* looks like shredded wheat and is baked with sesame, almonds and honey. *Sütlaç* (rice pudding) is definitely more delicious than anything you had in childhood. Ice cream (*dondurma*) is high quality, too. Two delicacies from the harem will please you as much as they did the palace lovelies: "lady's navel" (*hanım göbeği*), a creamy doughnut, and "beloved's lips" (*dilber dudağı*), almonds, walnuts, honey and rose syrup.

Drinks

Mineral water is readily available—sparkling (*maden suyu*) or plain (*memba suyu*). The beer is good, notably the national Efes Pilsen or locally produced Tuborg. *Rakı*, the aniseed-flavoured apéritif, customarily accompanies starters; it can be drunk diluted with water and ice or straight, with water (or beer) on the side. Turkish wines (*şarap*) have been produced since earliest antiquity; the Turks drink them in moderate quantities but uninhibited by the strictures of Islam. The whites (*beyaz*) are probably best in quality, particularly with seafood, but the reds (*kırmızı*) and rosés (*roze*) are quite respectable. Slightly alcoholized grape juice (*şıra*) is also popular, as are fruit juices (*meyva suyu*): freshly squeezed grapefruit or orange are best of all.

Turkish coffee (*kahve*) is more popular with discerning foreigners than with the Turks themselves. Ask for the strong thick brew sweet (*çok şekerli*), medium (*orta şekerli*) or without sugar (*sade*). The Turks prefer tea (*çay*), served in small tulip glasses, without milk.

The Hard Facts

To plan your trip, here are some of the practical details you should know about Turkey:

Airports

International and charter flights fly to Istanbul or, for travellers heading first for the Aegean coast, to Izmir. Both airports are located 25 km (15 miles) from the city centre.

Ankara's Esenboğa airport is some 30 km (18 miles) from the city centre.

In all cases, the airports provide the usual banking, car-hire and tourist information office services, in addition to duty-free shop, restaurant and snack bar facilities.

Climate

You'll enjoy the mildest, mellowest weather in spring and autumn, though Istanbul may be a little more humid than the breezy Aegean coast. Summers in both areas are hot and sticky, winters cool and rainy. A frequent feature of summers on the Aegean is the hot dry wind blowing up from the south.

Average noon temperatures from April to August rise in Istanbul from 12 to 23°C (54–74°F); on the coast from 16 to 27°C (61–80°F) and in Ankara from 10°C (51°F) to 23°C (73°F). In the autumn, they range around 20°C (68°F) in Istanbul, 22°C (71°F) on the coast, 14°C (57°F) in Ankara.

Communications

Put your holiday postcards inside envelopes and the post office will send them faster, as letter mail. Turkey is progressively installing a modern telecommunication system for fax and phone. Call worldwide with phone cards *(telekart)* from street phones, much cheaper than the hotel's surcharge service. For e-mail facilities, Internet cafés have sprung up right across the country, even in the smallest village.

Crime

Turkey generally poses no problem for personal security, and people are predominantly honest. Pickpockets—very often a fellow tourist—may be a problem in the bazaars, street markets or crowded public transport. Without being paranoid, don't tempt them with an open handbag or a wallet in the hip pocket. Put valuables in the hotel safe. Drug offences are severely punished by long prison sentences.

Driving

Before deciding to rent a car, you should know that Turkish drivers are frenetically impatient and have one of the highest accident rates in the Mediterranean region. Driving in Istanbul, Ankara or other big town is more trouble than it's worth. In any case, be sure you have a valid national licence or International Driving Permit. Rental age limit is over 21. To avoid unpleasant surprises, check on the exact extent of varying insurance coverages, personal, fire, collision, theft, etc. Drive on the right, overtake on the left, drive defensively but not at a provocative snail's pace.

Electric Current

All appliances need double round-pin plugs for 220-volt, 50-cycle A.C.

Embassies

The embassies are in Ankara. Most countries also have a consulate in Istanbul.

British Embassy
Sehit Ersan Caddessi 46A
Cankaya, Ankara
Tel. (312) 455 3344
Fax (312) 455 3356

US Embassy
Atatürk Bulvar 110
Kavaklidere 06100, Ankara
Tel. (312) 455 5555
Fax (312) 467 0019

Emergencies

Most problems can be handled at your hotel desk, but for real emergencies telephone: police **155**, ambulance **112**, fire brigade **110**. Consular help is there only for critical situations, lost passports or worse, *not* for lost cash or plane tickets.

Essentials

You won't need much formal wear. Pack a sun hat and add a sweater for cool evenings. Good walking shoes are vital, especially for archaeological sites, and easy-to-kick-off sandals or moccasins for the mosques—headscarves for women. Include insect repellent and a pocket torch (flashlight).

Formalities

Citizens of most countries need only a valid passport, but US, British and Irish citizens, and some other nationals, must purchase a visa at point of entry. The fee varies according to nationality (currently Australia US$20; Irish Republic €10; Canada US$45; Great Britain £10; USA US$100) for a maximum stay of 3 months with multiple entries.

Customs controls are minimal at point of entry, with an official duty-free import allowance of 200 cigarettes and 50 cigars or 200 g tobacco, 1 litre or 1 bottle of wine and/or spirits and 5 120-ml bottles of perfume. It is possible to purchase in addition 400 cigarettes, 100 cigars and 500 g pipe tobacco from the Turkish Duty Free shops on entering the country. The are no limits on the amounts of local or foreign currency imported, but foreign currencies should be declared and specified in your passport on arrival. Visitors may export up to US$5000 or equivalent in local or foreign currencies on departure, and amounts in excess if they have been declared and registered on arrival.

Important valuables such as expensive jewellery or electronic equipment may be noted on a form accompanying your passport to avoid difficulties on departure.

Health

Apart from minor stomach upsets from change of diet, the big health hazard in Turkey is the sun. Watch out for sunstroke, heat exhaustion and dehydration. Stick to the shade, wear a hat, use a good sun screen, drink plenty of water, it's as simple as that. To be on the safe side, stick to bottled mineral water.

For emergencies, make sure your health insurance covers holiday illnesses, as Turkey's social security does not extend to foreign visitors. Doctors, dentists and hospital staff in Istanbul and other large towns are well trained, and most speak good English or German. If you expect to need prescription medicines, take your own supply as you may not find the exact equivalent on the spot. In an emergency, you'll find good anti-diarrhoea pills at the pharmacy (eczane). You must take protection against mosquitoes during the summer months.

Language

English and German have gradually replaced French as the Turks' second language. Except for hotels or other tourist establishments, do not expect to find anything but Turkish spoken outside Istanbul, Ankara and major resorts.

Media

Most European newspapers and European editions of American dailies are available, a day or so late, in Istanbul and major resorts. The Turkish Daily News is published in English.

Many hotels receive BBC World Service, Sky News or CNN television by satellite. BBC and Voice of America radio are 69 accessible on short wave. Turkish state radio and TV also have English, German and French language news programmes.

Money

The national unit of currency is the Yeni Türk Lirası (new Turkish lira, YTL), divided into 100 new kurus (Ykr). Coins are issued in denominations of 1, 5, 10, 25, 50 Ykr and 1 YTL; banknotes of 1, 5, 10, 20, 50, 100 YTL. The old lira, with six extra zeros, is valid until end 2005, and until then all prices are given in old and new lira.

Most major shops and restaurants in Istanbul and Ankara welcome credit cards, as well as travellers cheques. Keep all receipts carefully. Smaller establishments prefer cash. Money and travellers cheques can be exchanged at all PTT branches. Travellers cheques are cashed immediately upon proof of identity; to avoid extra charges it is advised to take travellers cheques in pounds sterling, euros or US dollars.

ATM cash distributors for all international credit cards are common in the bigger towns.

Opening hours

The following times are subject to variations:

Banks generally open Monday to Friday 8.30 a.m.–noon and 1.30–5 p.m.; in tourist areas, they open weekends as well.

Shops are open non-stop from around 8 or 8.30 a.m. to 7 or 8 p.m., later in some bazaars. Sunday is the usual closing day, but by no means compulsory everywhere.

Main post offices open Monday to Saturday 8 a.m. to 8 p.m., Sundays 9 a.m.–7 p.m.

Museums, palaces and archaeological sites usually close on Mondays only (except Topkapı, closed Tuesday).

Photography

Film for video or still-cameras is readily available in Turkey. Choose film speeds appropriate to the country's brilliant Mediterranean light.

Most museums, palaces and archaeological sites allow you to take photographs, but usually for an extra fee, and with restrictions on the use of flash. Avoid photographing Muslims at prayer. For other, equally obvious reasons, avoid taking pictures of areas involving military security—airports, naval bases or border crossings.

Public Holidays

Turkey's public holidays are:

January 1	New Year's Day
April 23	National Independence and Children's Day

May 19   Youth and Sports
          Day (Atatürk's Day)
August 30 Victory Day, 1922
          war with Greeks
October 29 Republic Day

The Festival of Ramadan *(Ramazan)*, the ninth month in Muslim lunar calendar, is not an official holiday but is observed by the faithful with fasting and prayer, particularly in conservative Anatolian towns. Many shops and bazaars close on *Ramazan Bayramı* (end of Ramadan) and, just over two months later, on *Kurban Bayramı* (Feast of the Sacrifice).

Public Transport

Istanbul's buses cater less to tourists than to the needs of the year-round residents, so that you will not generally find them convenient for sightseeing on your own. The tram system is more useful, one line running between the Eminönü ferry landings, Sultanahmet and the Beyazıt district of the Grand Bazaar, the other running the length of Beyoğlu's main thoroughfare, Istiklâl Caddesi, to and from Taksim Square.

Taxis run on the meter, so you should not have to haggle over fares, but write down your destination as the driver rarely speaks anything other than Turkish. Shared taxis, *dolmuş,* run on specific routes, letting you off wherever you want for a pre-set fare.

They are much cheaper than an ordinary taxi and more fun if you don't mind being squashed.

Best of all are the ferries serving the Golden Horn, Bosphorus, Üsküdar and Princes' Islands from Eminönu and Sirkeci piers east of Galata Bridge. On the timetables, ports on the European shore are printed in black, on the Asian shore in red.

In Anatolia, long-distance buses from the *otogar* (bus station) are privately owned and highly competitive. Only the more expensive companies offer buses with non-smoking or air-conditioning.

Tipping

Service is included in hotel and restaurant bills, but you can always add a little extra. Apart from hairdressers or private tour-guides, tipping is much less customary than you might imagine and you should respect polite refusals.

Toilets

Men have fewer problems than women, but if you don't want to "go Turkish", take advantage of the facilities at hotels or tourist restaurants. In some places toilet paper may not be provided so carry a spare roll in your bag. It should be placed in the containers beside the toilet, not flushed away, as it might block the pipes. 71

INDEX

Alacahöyük 52
Amasya 52–54
Anadolu Hisarı 33
Ankara 44–49
Aphrodisias 42
Assos 36
Ayvalık 36
Bodrum 43
Bosphorus 32–33
Bursa 33–34
Çeşme 38
Didyma 41
Ephesus 39–41
Gallipoli 34
Gordion 55–56
Hattuşaş 49–51
Istanbul 17–30
  Aqueduct of Valens 25–26
  Archaeology Museum 23
  Basilica Cistern 20
  Blue Mosque 20
  Burnt Column 23
  Büyük Çamlıca 30
  Byzantine ramparts 26–27
  Church of St Saviour in Chora (Kariye Camii) 26
  Çirağan Palace 32
  Dolmabahçe Palace 29–30
  Eminönü 24–25
  Eyüp Mosque (see Golden Horn) 25
  Florence Nightingale Museum 30
  Galata Tower 27–28
  Golden Horn 25
  Grand Bazaar 23
  Hippodrome 19
  Istiklâl Caddesi 28–29
  Kumkapı district 26
  Mihrimah Mosque 30
  Military Museum 29
  Mosque of Suleiman the Magnificent 24
  Museum of the Ancient Orient 23
  Museum of Turkish and Islamic Art 22–23
  Pera Palace Hotel 28
  Rüstem Paşa Mosque 25
  Spice Market 25
  St Sophia 18–19
  Sultanahmet Camii 19–20
  Taksim Square 29
  Theodosian Walls 26–27
  Topkapı Palace 20–22
  Yeni Valide Mosque 30
Izmir 37–38
Kangal 55
Kuşadası 39
Marmaris 43
Miletus 41
Pamukkale 41–42
Pergamum 36–37
Pessinus 56–57
Priene 41
Princes' Islands 32
Rumeli Hisarı 33
Safranbolu 57
Selçuk 39–41
Sivas 54–55
Tokat 54
Troy 35–36
Yazılıkaya 51–52

GENERAL EDITOR
Barbara Ender-Jones
EDITING
Alice Taucher
LAYOUT
Luc Malherbe
PHOTO CREDITS
Bernard Joliat: pp. 1, 2, 6, 11, 31, 38, 45;
Hémisphères/Guiziou: p. 2;
Hémisphères/Frances: pp. 53, 62
Huber/Schmid: pp. 16, 21, 33, 42
Huber/Simeone: p. 18
Andrew Wheeler: p. 61;
Dominique Michellod: p. 64
MAPS
JPM Publications
Elsner & Schichor

Printed in Switzerland – 05/04/01
Weber/Bienne
Edition 2005–2006